101
Nature
Experiments

101
Nature
Experiments

Written by
DAVID BURNIE

DK

A DK PUBLISHING BOOK

Editor Helena Spiteri
Designers Susan St. Louis, Ivan Finnegan
US editor Camela Decaire
Managing editor Gillian Denton
Managing art editor Julia Harris
Assistant editor Susila Baybars
Picture research Deborah Pownell
Production Catherine Semark
Special photography Andy Crawford, Steve Gorton

First American edition 1996
2 4 6 8 10 9 7 5 3 1

Published in the United States by DK Publishing, Inc.,
95 Madison Avenue, New York, NY 10016

Published in Great Britain by Dorling Kindersley Limited

Distributed by Houghton Mifflin Company, Boston

A CIP catalog record is available from the Library of Congress

ISBN 0-7894-0466-4

Color reproduction by Colourscan, Singapore
Printed in Singapore by Toppan

Be a safe naturalist
• **Always** follow the steps in each experiment carefully.
• **Be careful**, especially when handling hot or heavy objects.
• **Make sure** you clean up after each experiment.

This sign means that extra caution is needed.
Ask an adult to help you.

This sign means that you should never disturb an
animal in its home or take it away from its natural habitat.

Contents

THE WORLD AROUND US

LIFE IN WATER

LIFE IN SOIL

PLANTS AND GROWTH

THE WORLD AROUND US

THE WORLD IS FULL of many kinds of living things. Some can move around, while others spend their lives rooted in one place. A few are taller than a house, and some are so tiny that they can only be seen with a microscope. Despite all these differences, living things do have some features in common. They all need oxygen and water to survive, and they are all made up of tiny units called cells.

1 Is air really there?

Air is all around us. When it moves, it presses against everything in its path. But unless it is blowing, we seldom feel that it is actually there. In this experiment you will see air at work. By sealing a funnel to a glass jar, you will see what happens when water tries to get in without air being able to get out.

You will need:

Funnel with a narrow tube   Plasticine   Pencil

Pitcher of water   Glass jar

1. Put the funnel in the mouth of the jar and mold a layer of plasticine around the join.

2. Make sure that you have enough plasticine to circle the jar. Press the plasticine firmly to seal it against the funnel and the jar. When you have done this, look carefully to make sure there are no gaps where air could escape.

3. Slowly pour some water into the funnel. If the funnel is narrow enough, you may find that a little water trickles through, but the water will soon stop. The rest of the water stays in the funnel, even though its end is open.

If you color the water you will see it more clearly.

Air pushes on the water in the funnel and holds it there.

Hole made by pencil

4. The water cannot get into the jar because the jar is already full of air that cannot get out.

5. Carefully make a hole through the plasticine with the pencil. Slowly remove the pencil, and watch what happens next.

6. The air can now escape from the jar. As soon as this happens, the water pours into the jar, taking up the space the air once filled.

3 See a plant drink

Plants suck up water through tiny pipelines in their roots and stems and let it evaporate (turn into a vapor) through microscopic holes in their leaves and flowers. Water helps a plant grow and keep its cells firm, so it does not wilt. In this experiment you will see how water moves up a stem into a flower. The food coloring shows where the water goes.

👫 *Adult supervision is advised*

Water has traveled up the stem to the petals.

You will need:

Tape

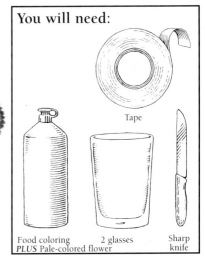

Food coloring
PLUS Pale-colored flower

2 glasses

Sharp knife

1. Fill the glasses with water. Add some food coloring to one of them and stir it well.

2. Lay the flower on a work surface and carefully slice its stem in two. Work from the bottom of the stem, stopping halfway up.

Tape prevents stem from splitting.

3. Wind some tape around the end of the cut to prevent the stem from splitting further.

4. Put each stem half into a glass. Lean the flower against a wall or window.

5. Within an hour, the dye should begin to color one half of the flower.

2 Test your breath

When you breathe, your body gives up water to the air outside. The water you breathe out forms an invisible vapor. When your warm breath hits a cold mirror, you will see it turn back into a liquid.

You will need:

Mirror

Put the mirror in the fridge for an hour. Wipe it, hold it close to your mouth, and breathe on it. Water vapor in your breath turns into drops of water, making the mirror turn misty. The colder the mirror, the more easily drops form.

7

4 Measure water loss through a leaf

Every day a tree sucks up water from the soil and lets it evaporate from its leaves. But how much water vapor actually escapes from a single leaf? In this experiment you will measure the amount of water some leaves give off, and divide it by their surface area.

You will need:

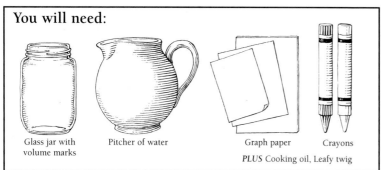

Glass jar with volume marks

Pitcher of water

Graph paper

Crayons

PLUS Cooking oil, Leafy twig

1. Fill a jar with water and add a thin layer of oil. Put the twig in the water and note the water level. After eight hours check the water level and see how much water has disappeared.

Leaf area is estimated by adding up the squares.

2. Use a crayon to draw an outline of each leaf on graph paper and add up the squares inside each outline. Divide the amount of water lost by the number of squares. This shows how much water is lost by each square of the leaf.

The oil seals off the water, making sure it can only escape through the leaves.

5 Rot a pepper

In nature nothing is ever wasted. As soon as something dies, it is broken down by other living things, such as molds and bacteria. This process is called decay, or rotting. Slice open a ripe and juicy red pepper or tomato. Leave it for two weeks and see what happens.

Adult supervision is advised

Day one

Day eight

Slice a red pepper in two. Over the next two weeks, observe how mold spreads over the pepper, making it rot.

Day fifteen

6 Natural recycling

Vegetable peelings and leftovers are not very appetizing. But instead of throwing them away, why not put them to good use? If you make a compost heap, you can recycle this kind of waste and turn it into a valuable fertilizer for garden plants.

You will need:

Screwdriver or hammer

Screws or nails *PLUS* Brackets, Kitchen and garden waste

Trowel

Four pieces of plywood, each about 20 in (50 cm) square

Adult supervision is essential

1. Ask an adult to help you make a square box from the plywood and brackets. Stand the box in a corner of a garden or backyard.

2. Gradually fill the box with waste you collect, such as peelings and leftovers from the kitchen and weeds from the garden.

3. As the heap builds up, the waste will start to break down. This will happen faster if you keep the heap in a warm and damp place.

Petals

Banana skin

Weeds

Cabbage

Flowers

Vegetable peelings and waste

4. After several weeks the compost should be ready. You can spread it in a garden to help the plants grow.

Decomposed waste makes excellent fertilizer.

Mature compost heap

7 Make animal cells

Cells are tiny compartments that make up all living things. Animals have many different cells, and each one has a special job. Some cells enable an animal to move, while others allow it to sense its surroundings. Here you will make a model that resembles a group of animal cells living together.

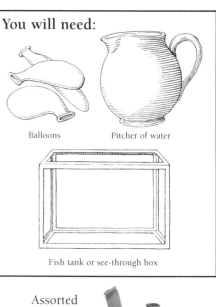

You will need:

Balloons   Pitcher of water

Fish tank or see-through box

1. Place the tank and balloons on a tabletop. The tank represents a tiny part of an animal's body, the balloons its cells.

Assorted colored balloons

2. Fit the mouth of each balloon around a faucet. Slowly fill the balloons with water. Be careful not to fill the balloons too much.

3. Hold each balloon by the neck. Knot the ends to seal the water inside, then gently place them in the tank.

Real animal cells are surrounded by fluid.

5. Pour in enough water to cover the balloons. In a living animal, fluid keeps the cells alive. Now your model resembles a tiny group of animal cells.

4. Keep adding balloons until the tank is full. The balloons must be tightly packed together with only a little space in between.

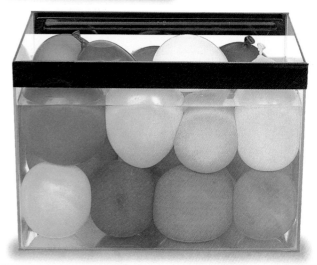

8 See plant cells

Plant cells are not the same as animal cells. Instead of being soft and flexible, they have a tough outer wall that gives them a fixed shape. Some plant cells are much bigger than animal cells, which makes them easier to see. In this experiment you will use a magnifying glass to see cells in an onion.

Adult supervision is advised

You will need:

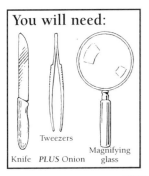

Knife *PLUS* Onion

Tweezers

Magnifying glass

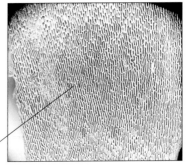

Onion cells as seen through a microscope at low magnification.

1. Cut a small square out of an onion. Using the tweezers, pull away a thin film of onion skin. Press it onto a windowpane so it sticks in position. You should now be able see its cells with the magnifying glass.

In a living animal, fluid keeps the cells alive.

9 How sugar moves water

Cells must have water to survive. They get water by soaking it up from their surroundings. In this experiment you will see how raisin cells take in water. The cells in each raisin are dead, but they do contain lots of sugar. The sugar helps suck in water from outside.

You will need:

Saucer of raisins

Pitcher of water   Glass jar   Spoon

Raisins

1. Press some raisins between your fingertips. They should feel dry and hard. Now spoon them into a jar.

Swollen raisins

2. Add enough water so you almost fill the jar. Even though the raisins are now underwater, they still look very dry and shriveled.

3. Stir the raisins and leave them in the jar. The sugar in the raisin cells will slowly draw in some of the water.

4. After three hours, look at the jar again. The cells have taken in so much water that the raisins are now swollen and plump.

10 Living together

Where can you find the biggest variety of plants and animals? Which things often live side by side? Find out the answers to these questions by using a wooden square called a quadrat. A quadrat is a device that is used to mark out a patch of ground in order to survey wildlife in different habitats.

Quadrat divides the plants into measured squares.

11 How salt moves water

In the experiment opposite, water moves in to cells containing sugar. Here, find out what happens when water moves the other direction. This experiment uses potatoes, which contain living cells. Salt helps draw water out of the cells.

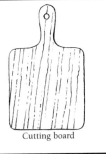

1. Cut the potatoes into large pieces and remove the skin. Notice how hard the potato feels.

2. Fill the two bowls with water. Add some salt to one bowl, but leave the other as it is.

3. Stir the salt to help it dissolve. Don't worry if some is left at the bottom of the bowl.

Cubed potatoes

4. Add some pieces of potato to each bowl. Leave them for about two hours. Then pick them up and compare them.

5. The cells in salty surroundings have lost water, making the potato feel soft and rubbery. The cells in pure water are unchanged.

1. Assemble and screw the pieces of wood together to make a square frame. Using a ruler and pencil, divide each side into quarters. Stretch the string across the quarter marks and fasten it with the tacks. The frame is now divided into 16 squares.

2. Put the frame on the ground and record the plants and animals in each small square on some graph paper.

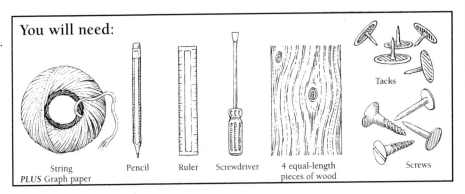

LIFE IN WATER

ALL PLANTS AND ANIMALS need water to survive. About three-quarters of our planet is covered with water. Most of it is salty, and makes up the seas and oceans. The rest is freshwater, found in streams and rivers, and comes from rain. Unlike seawater, it contains little or no salt. Freshwater makes up only a fraction of the water on our planet, but it is an important habitat for wildlife.

12 Filter water

When it rains, some water goes into streams and rivers, the rest sinks into the ground. As rain moves through holes in rock and soil, it gets filtered, and by the end of its journey it is clean. In this experiment you will see how this filtering process works.

You will need:

Cupful of coarsely broken charcoal
Cupful of rinsed sand
Cupful of washed gravel

Coffee filter paper or blotting paper

Pitcher of pondwater

Flowerpot

Sieve

Large dish

1. Line a flowerpot with filter paper. Fill a third of it with charcoal. Rinse some sand in a sieve and pack it on the charcoal. Fill the rest of the flowerpot with gravel.

2. Collect some pondwater in a pitcher. Hold the sieve over the flowerpot, and gently pour the dirty pondwater through it in a steady steam.

The sand inside traps small pieces of dirt.

The charcoal and filter paper trap tiny particles of dirt.

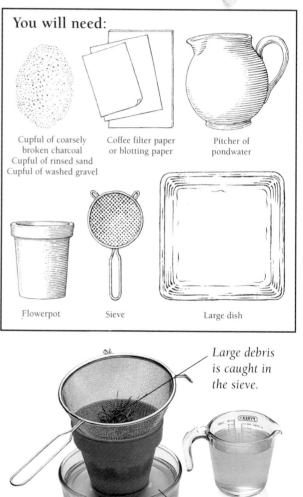

Large debris is caught in the sieve.

Filtered water collects in the dish.

3. Wait until all the pondwater has passed through the layers of charcoal, sand, and gravel. Then remove the flowerpot from the tray and pour the water back into the pitcher. The water is now much cleaner. But do not drink it!

13 Train fish with sound

Fish can hear sounds from outside a fish tank. If you have some goldfish, you can carry out this simple experiment in animal behavior and see how fish will learn to associate sound with food.

You will need:

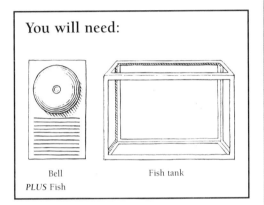

Bell
PLUS Fish
Fish tank

Set up a regular routine of ringing a bell just before you feed the fish. If you do this for several days, you will find that the fish learn the sound of the bell means food. As soon as they hear it, they will expect to eat.

14 Make an aquarium

A freshwater aquarium is like an indoor pond. Fill it with plants and animals that normally live together, and you can see how they feed and grow. Put the tank somewhere bright, but keep it away from direct sunlight so the water does not get too warm.

You will need:

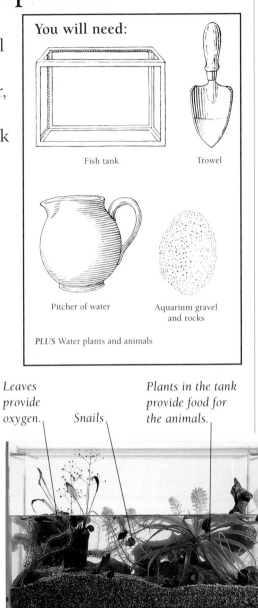

Fish tank
Trowel

Pitcher of water
Aquarium gravel and rocks

PLUS Water plants and animals

1. Rinse the gravel and then spread it out in a layer on the base of the tank. Next, add rocks, so the animals have somewhere to hide and a surface on which to feed.

2. Add enough water to half-fill the tank. Use rainwater – or better still, use water from a pond. Add rooted plants in their pots, or plant them in the gravel. Add pond weed directly to the water.

Leaves provide oxygen.
Snails
Plants in the tank provide food for the animals.

3. Your aquarium is now ready to receive its animal inhabitants. If you have filled the tank with pond water, you may find that it already contains tiny floating animals. If you add some pond snails, they will scrape tiny plants off the rocks and glass, and help keep the tank clean. If you decide to add some fish, remember to feed them, or they will soon eat all the tank's smaller inhabitants.

15 Going green

In nature, pure water is hard to find. It nearly always contains dissolved chemicals and tiny organisms. The water we drink is different, as most of these things have been removed. In this experiment you will compare three types of water to see how many microscopic plants they contain.

You will need:

3 glass jars

Pond water, filtered water, and tap water
PLUS Liquid plant fertilizer

1. Fill each glass jar with a different kind of water. Add a single drop of plant fertilizer to each one to encourage plant growth.

2. Leave the jars on a sunny windowsill for a few days. In the sunshine, the invisible water plants will slowly start to multiply.

Pond water turns green when plant fertilizer is added.

3. Look at the jars. Compare the color of the water in each one. The water that contained tiny plants will slowly turn green. The water that had few or no plants will stay clear much longer.

16 Walking on water

Did you know that water has a "skin"? Some small insects, called water striders, are so light they can walk across this skin without sinking. You can see the skin for yourself. It is known as surface tension, and is a function of the molecules making up water.

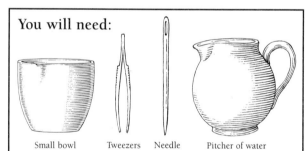

You will need:

Small bowl   Tweezers   Needle   Pitcher of water

1. Fill the bowl with water and wait until the surface is completely still.

2. Pick up the needle with the tweezers. Hold the needle horizontally so that it is level with the water's surface. Lower it slowly until it touches the water.

3. When the needle meets the water, open the tweezers. The needle should sit on the water's surface. If you break the water's skin, the needle will sink.

17 Trap underwater animals

In ponds, small animals often feed at night, when darkness hides them from their enemies. But strangely, the same animals are often attracted to light. In this experiment you can use light to lure some of these animals into a trap, and then examine them closely.

1. Tape the funnel to one end of the pipe, with the narrow end pointing into the tube. Switch on the flashlight and put it in the jar. Screw the lid on to stop water from coming in.

2. Put the jar in the pipe with the light shining through the funnel. Fasten the plastic over the open end of the pipe with the rubber bands.

3. Tie the string around both ends of the pipe, leaving it slack in the middle to make a handle. Lower it into the pond carefully and leave it there overnight.

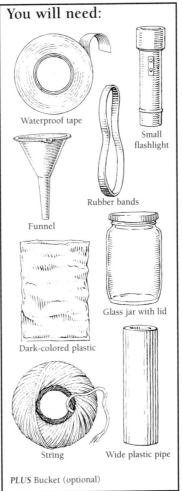

You will need:

Waterproof tape

Small flashlight

Funnel

Rubber bands

Glass jar with lid

Dark-colored plastic

String

Wide plastic pipe

PLUS Bucket (optional)

4. In the morning, pull up the trap, remove the black plastic, and pour the water inside the pipe into the bucket. Examine what you have caught. Put the animals back in the pond when you have finished.

18 Make a tide pool viewer

Coastal tide pools are like tiny worlds teeming with life. Each one has plants and animals that live there permanently, regularly cut off by the tide. These must adapt to varying conditions – the pool often heats up when the tide is out, and then cools down as fresh water spills in. With the help of this device, you can get a clear view of the inhabitants of a tide pool.

👥 *Adult supervison is advised*

You will need:

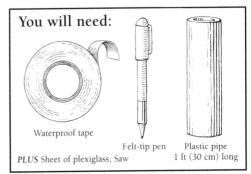

Waterproof tape

Felt-tip pen

Plastic pipe 1 ft (30 cm) long

PLUS Sheet of plexiglass, Saw

Put one end of the pipe on the plexiglass and draw around it with the pen. Ask an adult to cut out the circle with a saw. Tape this to one end of the pipe, making sure there are no gaps where water might be able to get in.

Small animals swim in through the wide spout of the funnel, but cannot find their way out.

\With your viewer you might see sea anemones and starfish like these.

19 Make a beachcomber's showcase

There is always plenty to do at the seashore. You can paddle in the water, explore the beach in search of plants and seashore wildlife, and collect plenty of colorful shells and pebbles. Here you will find out how to make an attractive showcase to display the shells that you find.

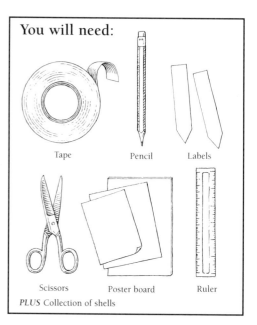

You will need:

Tape   Pencil   Labels

Scissors   Poster board   Ruler

PLUS Collection of shells

1. With the help of a ruler, cut out 16 strips of poster board that are 1 in (2.5 cm) wide.

Collection of shells

Lines are produced as the shell grows.

2. Take a fresh sheet of poster board, and draw a rectangle as long as the strips. Add a margin of 1 in (2.5 cm) around it, and then cut it out.

3. Fold up the margin around the rectangle to make four sides. Fasten them upright with some tape.

4. Use the strips of poster board to partition the case into small sections. You will need to cut slots in the strips to make them fit together.

5. Stick each strip to the edge of the showcase. Now you are ready to fill the showcase with your favorite shells.

6. Label each of your shells. Write down what kind it is, and the date and place you found it.

Protect the natural world

Clever collector
Only collect empty shells that are washed up on the beach. Don't be tempted to collect shells that still contain living animals because they will soon die.

All sorts of shells
Apart from the beach, you can find different kinds of empty shells in woods, parks, and beside the edges of ponds or streams. You might even find some in a garden.

Some shells are fragile, so handle them with care.

20 See inside a shell

Shells are portable homes made by animals such as cockles and snails. Some shells are shaped like saucers, but others are wound up in a tight spiral, making it very difficult to look inside. If you use some sandpaper, you can scrape holes in shells and see how they are built.

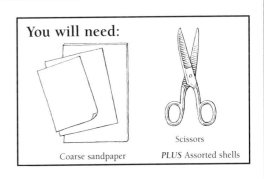

You will need:

Coarse sandpaper   Scissors   *PLUS* Assorted shells

Collection of shells

1. Cut a piece of sandpaper. Hold the shell against the sandpaper and rub it backward and forward. Be sure to keep your fingers out of the way.

2. After a while, the sandpaper will rub right through the shell. You will soon see a spiral chamber where the shell's inhabitant lived.

21 Make a mini pond

Making a pond is a great way to attract water wildlife into your garden. A big pond can be home to many different plants and animals, but if you don't have much room, a mini pond is almost as good. Here you can find out how to make a mini pond from a bucket or shallow bowl. If you add some water plants to your mini pond, you should attract some small water animals.

Pondweed

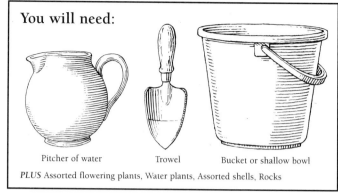

You will need:

Pitcher of water   Trowel   Bucket or shallow bowl

PLUS Assorted flowering plants, Water plants, Assorted shells, Rocks

1. Find an open and sunny spot in which to place the pond. Dig a hole that is as deep as the bucket.

3. Press the loose soil around the bucket so there are no gaps. Now you are ready to decorate it to make it look more natural.

5. Fill the pond with water. You can use tapwater, but it is better to use rainwater if you can collect enough. Add some rocks to the pond so that the water animals have somewhere to hide. Build them up the sides until they reach the rim so that any animals that fall in will have a way out. Now add some water plants.

2. Lower the empty bucket into the hole, making sure that it fits snugly. The rim should be level with the soil.

4. Take the flowering plants out of their pots and plant them around the edge of the pond. Add a few shells and pebbles in between.

Life in the pond
The plants will help supply oxygen to the water. As the weeks go by, they will attract small animals, such as damselflies. They fly to ponds and lay their eggs in the water. Many insects start life in the water and only take to the air when they become adults.

22 Test water for acidity

3 glass jars

Labels

Strips of litmus paper

Pen

Pitcher of water
Pitcher of vinegar

Notebook

Plants and animals that live in water are easily harmed when pollution in the air makes the water acidic. This happens when poisonous gases from cars or factories spread through the air. When rainwater falls through the gases, it becomes acidic. In this experiment you will make your own acid water with a little vinegar, and then use strips of litmus paper to test it. If water contains acid, litmus paper will show it by changing color. Continue the experiment by testing rainwater and the water from a pond to see if they are acidic.

1. Fill the first jar with tapwater and label it. Pour enough water into the second jar to make it three-quarters full, then top it up with vinegar. Label it "Slightly acidic."

2. Fill the third jar with an equal amount of water and vinegar. This mixture is more concentrated than the one in the second jar, so label it "Very acidic."

3. Now dip the litmus paper into each jar and write down the results in your notebook. The litmus paper turns pink when it soaks up water containing vinegar (regardless of how much vinegar is in the water). The litmus paper darkens slightly in tapwater because it is wet.

Strips of litmus paper

Litmus paper darkens slightly.

Jar of water

Litmus paper turns pink in slightly acid water.

"Slightly Acidic"

"Very acidic"

Litmus paper turns pink in very acidic water.

LIFE IN SOIL

THERE IS A HIDDEN WORLD of living things in the soil beneath our feet. Some of them creep or scuttle among the fallen leaves. Others dig burrows, or eat their way through the ground. Here you can find out about the living world in the soil and, with the help of some simple equipment, meet some of its tiny inhabitants.

23 Test the soil

The quality of soil varies a great deal. In some places it is deep and rich, while in others, it is thin, dry, and dusty. Life in the soil also varies. For example, very few animals can survive in wet, acidic soil. But alkaline soil is rich in minerals and supports an abundance of life. In this experiment you will use litmus paper to test soil and see if it is acidic or alkaline.

You will need:

Soil

Spoon

Red litmus paper
Blue litmus paper

Distilled water

Jar with lid

1. Collect a small sample of soil and put a spoonful of it in a jar. Use the spoon to break up any big lumps.

Soil sample

2. Half-fill the jar with distilled water. This will dissolve the chemicals in the soil. Screw on the lid of the jar, making sure that it is tight.

3. Shake the jar well, for about a minute, to mix the soil and water. Leave the jar to stand on a flat surface until the soil has settled.

4. Place one strip of each litmus paper on the table. Unscrew the jar and dip the handle of the spoon into the mixture.

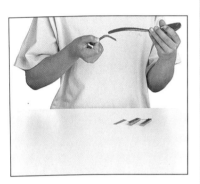

5. Dab the handle onto each of the paper strips so that each one is wetted. See which one of the litmus papers changes color.

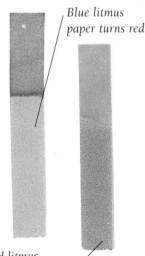

Blue litmus paper turns red

Red litmus paper turns blue

6. If the soil is acid, the red litmus paper turns blue. If the soil is alkaline, the blue litmus paper turns red.

24 Keeping cool

On a warm, sunny day, the surface of the soil soon heats up and gets too hot and dry for some soil animals. Beneath the surface, it is very different. Use a thermometer, and you will see that even when the surface of the soil is warm, the soil below the surface always remains cool.

1. Leave one of the thermometers aside to measure the temperature of the air. Then find a sunny patch in the yard and dig a small hole.

2. Push one thermometer into the surface of the soil. This will tell you the temperature of the top layer of soil.

3. Put the third thermometer into the hole you have dug. Then fill it with soil so that only the top of the thermometer is showing. Leave it for ten to fifteen minutes.

4. Now remove the thermometer and read it. You should find that the temperature beneath the surface of the soil is cooler than the temperature of the air, and much cooler than the temperature of the surface of the soil higher up. The coolness of the soil keeps small animals comfortable and stops them from getting too hot and drying out.

You will need:

3 thermometers   Trowel

Air is cooler than the surface of soil.

Hottest place is the surface of the soil.

Beneath the surface of the soil, it is even cooler than the air.

25 Make a pit trap

During the night, when we are asleep, many small animals are wide awake. They wander far and wide looking for food, but they move silently, and leave few signs that they have passed by. By the time we wake up, they have already hidden themselves away. If you want to see these animals, you don't have to stay up all night. Instead, you can make the simple pit trap shown here. It holds small animals without harming them, and lets you look at them during the day.

A piece of wood

Four large stones

A cube of cheese

Cookie crumbs

A piece of apple

A piece of meat

1. Dig a hole in the ground large enough to hold the glass jar. Pack the loose soil around the jar to hold it in place. Make sure that the rim is level with the ground's surface, so animals will fall in easily.

2. Put some bait in the jar. You can use the bait shown here, but any small scraps of leftover food will do, particularly those with strong smells. The smell of the bait will attract passing animals.

3. Put the large stones around the four corners of the trap, and place the wood or tile on top. This will prevent rain from getting into the trap and harming any animals that have been caught.

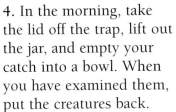

4. In the morning, take the lid off the trap, lift out the jar, and empty your catch into a bowl. When you have examined them, put the creatures back.

5. Now try varying the bait to see if different kinds of foods attract different animals. Try fruit and cookie crumbs one night, and then meat the next.

6. Set up several traps in different places to see if the types of visitors vary. Record your results in a notebook to find out where different creatures live.

Supporting stones

The cover stops big animals from eating the food.

Check trap during the day to see if day visitors differ from night visitors.

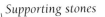

Small creatures cannot climb up the steep sides.

The smell of cheese attracts different animals.

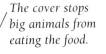

26 Look at life in the soil

The surface layers of soil are full of small creatures. Many of them feed on the remains of dead plants. Others are tiny hunters that search for their prey in the soil. Most soil animals hide away from light, which makes them hard to see. Here you will use light to make them come into the open.

You will need:

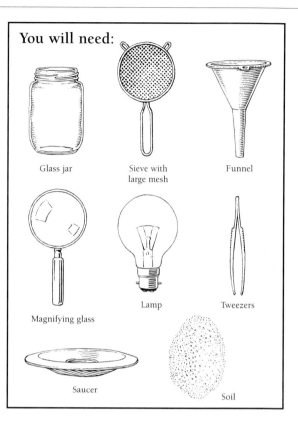

Glass jar

Sieve with large mesh

Funnel

Magnifying glass

Lamp

Tweezers

Saucer

Soil

Angled lamp is ideal for flexibility.

Make sure the sieve is firmly positioned in the funnel.

Tiny creatures can be seen easily with a magnifying glass.

1. Place the funnel in the glass jar. Add a small amount of soil to the sieve, then rest the sieve in the funnel. Bring the lamp close to the soil and switch it on. Leave the lamp shining on the soil for about half an hour. The light and warmth will drive tiny soil animals downward into the jar.

The animals emerge through the spout of the funnel.

2. Tip the animals into the saucer, separate them with the tweezers, and examine them using the magnifying glass. You will achieve different results if you use soil from different places, like a forest or a vegetable patch.

27 Make a worm farm

Earthworms are among the most important animals in the soil. As they eat their way through the soil, they help mix it up, improving its fertility. They bring minerals up from the bottom layers and take dead plant matter down from the top. Make a worm farm in a jar and you can see all this activity.

You will need:

Soil, Sand

Bowl

Spray bottle

Glass jar

Trowel

PLUS Leaves, Earthworms

1. Spray the soil and sand with water to make them moist. Build up separate layers until the jar is full. It is essential that the earthworms have plenty of moisture, so keep the layers damp.

3. Cover the worms with the leaves. Put the farm in a cool, dark place. Every few days, check the jar for activity.

2. Add the worms to the jar with care. Five or six worms should be enough to occupy a large glass jar.

Dead leaves

Sand

Soil

Leaves dragged down into soil

Soil

Earthworms

Layers of sand and soil merge from the activity of the earthworms.

Active worm farm

Worm tunnels

Leaves

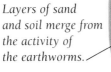

28 Running for cover

Most soil animals spend their lives hidden away, either under leaves or in the earth. This helps protect them from their enemies and stops their bodies from drying out. It also makes it difficult for us to see them. In this experiment you can see how soil animals react when their underground world suddenly changes. Some of them stay where they are, but others look for a safer hideout.

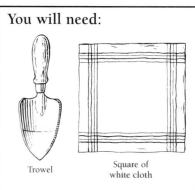

You will need:

Trowel

Square of white cloth

1. Put the square of cloth on the ground. Use the trowel to dig up a mixture of earth and weeds. Put this in the center of the cloth, spreading it out to form a thin layer.

2. Now watch to see what happens. You will probably see some animals moving across the cloth as they head for shelter. Spiders and centipedes usually act quickly, while slugs and snails react more slowly.

Keeping damp
We have thick skin, which keeps moisture in our bodies. But many soil animals have thin skin, so they depend on moisture in the soil to survive. If they are exposed, they can easily dry out and die.

Snail

Ladybug

29 What substances are in soil?

Imagine trying to make some soil. You would need lots of different ingredients – but what are they, and where would you get them? This experiment will help you find out. Soil is made of two main substances: minerals and organic matter. Minerals come from rocks and are found in the form of tiny stones or specks of grit that sink in water. The rest of soil is made up of humus, or organic matter, which often floats. Humus comes from the remains of plants and animals. When a soil sample is mixed with water it will separate into these substances, forming different layers according to their weight and size.

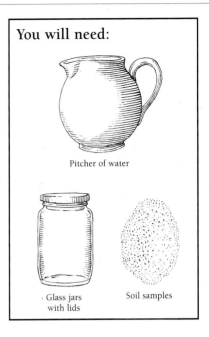

You will need:

Pitcher of water

Glass jars with lids

Soil samples

Mixture of earth and grass.

Put the cloth near earth that is covered by leaves.

1. Collect small quantities of soil from different places, such as in the woods or the backyard. Put a sample of each in the glass jars.

2. Add enough water to each jar to sufficiently cover the soil – about double its volume. Screw the lids on tightly. Mark each jar so you know where the soil comes from.

3. Shake each jar hard for about half a minute. This will separate the different substances in the soil so that they float or sink.

4. Leave the jars to stand for a few minutes. Most of the mineral particles will sink, while the organic matter will float. You will be able to see which kind of soil has the most organic matter.

PLANTS AND GROWTH

PLANTS ARE ABLE to live and grow on sunlight, water, and air. Light gives plants the energy they need. Air and water, together with chemicals from the soil, make up their building materials. In warm and wet places, some plants grow over 300 ft (90 m) tall! In cold places, others can take years to grow a tiny amount.

30 Detect the growing point

Grass is one of nature's most important plants. But have you ever wondered how it survives being eaten and cut by lawn mowers? Compare growing sprout and grass seedlings to find out.

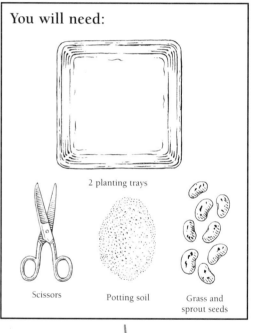

You will need:

2 planting trays

Scissors

Potting soil

Grass and sprout seeds

1. Fill both trays with the soil, and sow each with different seeds. When the seedlings are 2 in (5 cm) high, cut them at the base.

2. Watch what happens to the different plants. After a week, your sprout seedlings will not have grown back.

3. This box contains grass seedlings that are ready to be cut. They have quickly taken root and formed a dense mat of long, narrow leaves.

4. A week after you cut them, your grass seedlings will look like this. Instead of coming to a halt, they continue to grow. Grass plants can do this because they grow from a point very close to the ground. If their leaves are cut off, they grow up again. Sprout grows from a point at the top of the stem. If it is cut off below this, it is unable to grow back.

31 Watch seeds grow

A seed contains a tiny living plant, packed inside a very tough case. A seed also contains a store of food that can keep a plant alive for months, or even years. As long as the seed stays dry, the plant lies dormant, but as soon as it gets thoroughly wet, it starts to grow. Find out what amounts of water and air provide the best conditions for a plant to grow in this experiment.

You will need:

Bowl

3 saucers

Beans

Blotting paper

Pitcher of water

1. Soak the beans in water for 24 hours. This will get them very wet – just as heavy rain would if they were in the ground outside. The beans will be swollen after soaking. Drain and rinse them.

2. Put a piece of blotting paper on each saucer. Moisten the paper on one of the saucers and keep it damp, but not saturated, during the experiment.

3. Scatter some beans on each of the saucers and spread them out evenly.

4. Fill one of the saucers containing dry blotting paper with water so that the beans on it are completely covered and deprived of any air. Leave the last saucer without water.

DAY 5

Beans saturated with water do not have enough air to grow.

DAY 5

Only the beans that are left on damp paper germinate and grow.

Both water and air are needed for a plant to prosper.

32 Grow vegetable tops

Did you know that you can make some vegetables come to life? With the help of water and sunlight, you can watch as their tops begin to sprout new leaves and grow. This experiment works with all root vegetables, which include turnips, radishes, carrots, and parsnips.

☖☖ Adult supervision is advised

1. Place the turnip on the cutting board. You will only use the top, so you can eat what is leftover.

Watch the stem closely for any change.

2. Use the knife to cut off the top section of the turnip. The top contains the stem that produces new leaves.

4. Put the saucer on a sunny windowsill. Check the water level every day. As it evaporates, add more water.

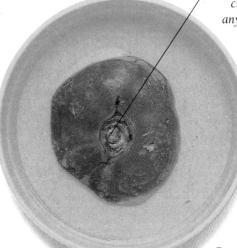

Day 1

After a few days, the new leaves appear as the turnip comes to life.

3. Place the turnip top in a saucer cut-end face-down. Add enough water to it so that it completely covers the cut surface.

Day 17

The leaves grow bigger, but the vegetable top cannot grow a new root.

Day 10

33 See a bean grow

This experiment lets you see what happens when a fava bean germinates and begins to grow. Normally, the bean would be hidden underground. By growing it in a glass, you can see exactly what happens in its first days of life.

You will need:

Scissors

Fava beans

Pencil

Cotton

Tall glass

Blotting paper
Graph paper

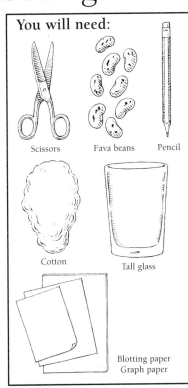

New leaves

Moist cotton

Graph

Strong roots anchor it in the glass.

1. Line the inside of a glass with blotting paper and pack in the cotton. Position the bean so it rests between the blotting paper and the glass.

2. Stick a strip of graph paper on the outside close to the bean. Half-fill the glass with water, set it aside, and wait for the bean to grow.

3. Use the graph paper to measure how much the bean grows each day. Keep the water level topped up so that the plant does not dry out.

34 Reaching for light

In order to grow, plants need light. They search this out as tirelessly as animals hunt for food. They sense light falling on their stems and react by growing toward it. Plant a climbing bean in a box with a hole in the top and you can watch it as it grows, reaching up toward the light.

You will need:

Tape

Scissors

Flowerpot

Potting soil

Matte black paint

Climbing beans

Cardboard

Paintbrush

PLUS Shoebox

1. Cut a small hole in one end of the box.

2. Cut out two pieces of cardboard as deep as the box, but not quite as wide. Tape them into the box as shown below.

3. Paint the inside of the box black. The black paint will help absorb any stray light that comes in.

4. Plant the bean in the pot. Water it, and then put it into the box, positioned upright with the hole at the top. Put the lid on the box.

5. Every day, remove the lid to see what is happening inside. Once the bean has germinated, it should find its own way out of the box.

Plant eventually emerges through the hole.

35 Freeze leaves

During the winter months, we stay indoors and we wear extra clothing to keep warm. But plants stay outside without protection whatever the weather is like. Some plants have built-in "antifreeze" to help them survive the cold weather. Others don't, and in very low temperatures, their leaves freeze. When they thaw out, they collapse. See what happens when you freeze two different leaves.

Lettuce leaf

Rhododendron leaves

You will need:

Lettuce leaf
Evergreen leaf such as a Privet, Laurel, or Rhododendron
A freezer

2. As the leaves warm up, any ice crystals will start to melt. See what happens to the leaves when they have completely thawed out.

1. Pick a leaf from an evergreen bush and a leaf from a head of lettuce. Put both leaves in the freezer and leave them there for about 20 minutes; this will make their temperatures drop below freezing. Then take the leaves out and lay them on a tabletop.

Thawed lettuce leaf becomes soft and mushy.

Frozen rhododendron leaves

Evergreen leaf keeps its shape.

Surviving the winter

Deciduous plants drop all their leaves in the fall and grow a new set in the spring. Evergreen plants have tough leaves that can withstand the winter frost.

Fair-weather plants

Lettuces are "annual" plants, they do not survive from one year to the next. They die when it gets cold, but their seeds live on, growing into new plants the following year.

Frozen lettuce leaf

36 Grow a bean upside down

The root of a plant sucks up water and minerals, and also helps anchor the plant firmly in the soil. Roots grow straight down because they respond to gravity. To see how this happens, grow a bean in a jar. As soon as the root appears, turn the bean upside down, and watch the root change direction.

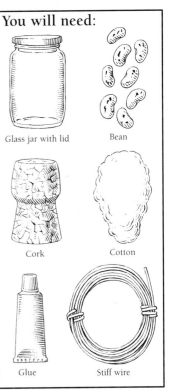

You will need:

Glass jar with lid

Bean

Cork

Cotton

Glue

Stiff wire

Roots grow downward in response to gravity.

Cork

Glue the cork inside the jar lid. Push the wire into the cork and thread the bean on it. Put damp cotton into the jar and screw on the lid. Once the root is ½ in (1 cm) long, rotate the jar 180°.

37 Test a potato for starch

When potato plants grow, they use sunlight to make a substance called starch. It is made in their leaves, but stored underground in swollen areas called tubers. Starch is a useful substance because it provides us with energy. In this experiment you can test a potato for starch using a chemical called iodine.

You will need:

Knife

Dropper

Iodine

PLUS Potato

👫 *Adult supervision is advised*

Slice a potato in half and then put a few drops of iodine onto the cut side. The iodine will turn from orange-brown to bluish-black. This reaction shows that the potato contains a large amount of starch.

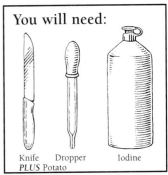

Blue-black iodine

38 Watch sap rise

In your body, blood carries dissolved substances from one place to another. Plants do not have blood, but they do use a liquid to move things around. This liquid is called sap. Normally, sap is hidden away inside a plant, but in this experiment you can see how sap oozes out when a stem is snapped.

You will need:

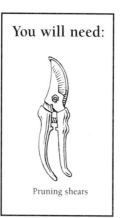

Pruning shears

⚠ *Adult supervision is advised*

1. Late spring is the best time of year to carry out this experiment. Trees are full of sap because they use the substances it contains to help them grow. Find a tree that has lots of young leafy branches. Carefully cut off one of the branches where it joins the tree. Examine the cut edge, and you should be able to see drops of sap seeping from the wood.

Sticky sap

Special sticky sap oozes out of cuts in the bark of some trees. It works like a liquid adhesive bandage, keeping insects and other animals away from the wood while the cut heals.

39 Grow an onion

Although it may look dead, an onion is very much alive. It is waiting for a chance to grow, but it must have water before it can start. In this experiment you will see what happens if you leave an onion in water.

You will need:

Glass jar

Pitcher of water

PLUS Onion

1. Fill a glass jar with water. Choose a large onion that feels firm and rest it in the mouth of the jar.

The bottom of the onion should touch the water.

2. After a few weeks, the onion will start to grow roots. These will spread downward through the water. Some time after the roots have appeared, the onion will start to grow leaves. If you take the onion out of the jar and place it in the ground, it might flower.

40 Discover root power

Although they are very small, young plants are amazingly strong. Their leaves can lift stones or pavement as they grow up toward the light, and their roots can fight their way down through the hardest soil in search of water and minerals. The end of a root is covered by a tiny cap that protects it as it grows. In this experiment you will see how roots are able to break their way out of an eggshell "flowerpot."

You will need:

Saucer

Potting soil

Teaspoon

Marigold seeds

Egg cup and eggshell

Pitcher of water

Half-eggshell

1. Using a teaspoon, carefully fill the half-eggshell to the top with some soil.

2. Put the shell in an egg cup and place it on a saucer. Sprinkle the seeds on the top and cover them with a little soil.

Do not let the soil get soggy.

3. Place in a warm, light place and water the soil every day. The seeds will germinate, and small shoots will appear in a few days.

Plant grows from the top of the eggshell.

Roots burst through the eggshell.

4. Lift up your miniature "flowerpot" and you will see that the roots have forced their way through the shell. Some roots are so strong that they can even push through cracks in rock.

41 Plant fruit pips

Some seeds are as small as specks of dust, but an avocado pit can be as big as a golf ball. If you plant it in a pot, you can grow an avocado plant of your own. Other fruits, such as oranges, apples, grapes, and peaches, also contain seeds or pips that you can plant and grow.

1. Soak the avocado pit in water for 24 hours. Put some soil in a bowl, add some water to make it moist. Stir the soil and put some into the flowerpots.

2. Plant the avocado pit, pointed end up, so it sticks out of the surface of the soil. Small fruit seeds should be buried, about ½ in (1 cm) deep in the soil.

3. Label the pots and cover with plastic bags. Secure the bags to prevent moisture from escaping and then put the pots in a warm, dark place.

Orange pips   Grape seeds

Apple pips

Peach pit

Avocado pit

4. After two to eight weeks, you should start to see signs of life. Take the pots out of the bags, and put them in a place with plenty of light.

Young new leaves

5. Keep the soil well watered and watch how your fruit trees grow. If roots begin to grow out of the bottom of any pot, it is time to move the plant to a new, bigger one.

The first leaves soon grow large.

42 Grow pots of vegetables

Even if you do not have a garden, you can become a vegetable gardener. You can grow vegetables in pots on your windowsill. The best kinds are those that climb and those that do not spread out too much. Root vegetables often need deep soil, so don't try and grow these unless you have space for very big pots.

You will need:

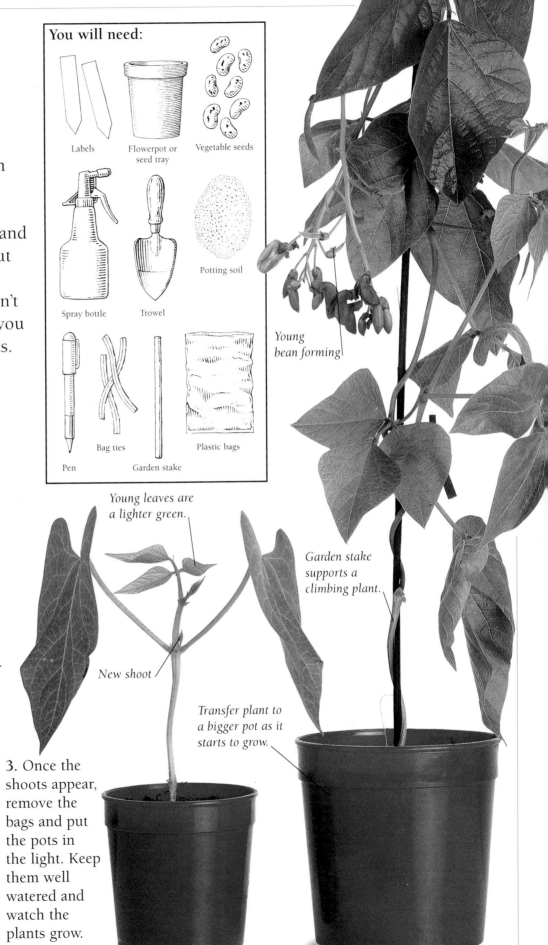

Labels

Flowerpot or seed tray

Vegetable seeds

Spray bottle

Trowel

Potting soil

Pen

Bag ties

Garden stake

Plastic bags

1. Fill some pots with soil. If you are growing plants that have small seeds, use a seed tray instead. This will make it easier to separate the seedlings.

2. Plant the seeds and spray the pots with water. Label and put them in plastic bags. Keep them in a warm, dark place to help germination.

3. Once the shoots appear, remove the bags and put the pots in the light. Keep them well watered and watch the plants grow.

Young leaves are a lighter green.

New shoot

Young bean forming

Garden stake supports a climbing plant.

Transfer plant to a bigger pot as it starts to grow.

43 Taking cuttings

Plants start life in several different ways. Many grow from seed, but some can also grow from snapped-off stems or single leaves. By taking cuttings, you can grow new plants without sowing seeds. Here you can find out how to grow cuttings in soil and in water.

You will need:

Flowerpot   Pitcher of water   Empty glass

Trowel   Bowl   Scissors   Potting soil
PLUS Cuttings

Growing plantlets
1. The plantlets at the end of a spider plant's runners have roots. When these are ½ in (1 cm) long, cut the plantlet off the runner.

2. Fill the flowerpot with some soil. Push the roots of the plantlet into the soil. Gently press down the soil around it so that the cutting is firmly in place.

Taking stem cuttings
1. Cut off a piece of stem about 4 in (10 cm) long, just below the leaf. Trim off the leaves to leave the stem three-quarters bare.

2. So that you can see how a cutting grows roots, put it into a glass of water instead of into soil. Keep the glass full, and once roots appear, plant the cutting in soil.

Taking care of your cuttings
Keep your cuttings away from direct sunlight and make sure that their soil is always damp. After a few weeks they should start to grow, showing that they have taken root.

Aluminum plant

Aeonium

Tradescantia

Spider plant

Painted-leaf Begonia

44 Grow sprout heads

Here is a growing experiment that turns plants into an unusual kind of hair! The "hair" is made of sprout seedlings and grows out of eggshell "flowerpots" that have their own painted faces. If you keep your sprout heads well watered, their hair will stand on end. But if you forget to water them, the cotton will dry out and their hair will start to flop in all different directions.

You will need:

Paint   Sprout seeds   Eggshells   Paintbrush

Glass of water   Cotton   Bowl of water

A handful of sprout seeds

Undecorated eggshell

1. Collect some halves of empty eggshells. Using a small brush, paint a face on each shell. Be sure to hold the shells gently or you might break them.

2. Break off a small piece of cotton. Moisten it in a bowl of water, then squeeze out any excess liquid and put it in one of the eggshells.

3. Scatter the sprout seeds on the surface of the damp cotton. Then put your sprout seeds somewhere light and warm and watch "hair" slowly grow.

Hair will grow in just a few days.

Keep cotton moist.

4. If you look at the experiment on page 30, you will find out why the hair will not grow back if you decide to give it a trim.

45 Make a mini desert

In deserts, months go by without rain, and the sunshine is fierce. Desert plants survive by having deep roots and by storing water in their fleshy stems. If you have a warm and sunny windowsill, you can make a desert of your own. Desert plants are easy to take care of because they do not need much water.

You will need:

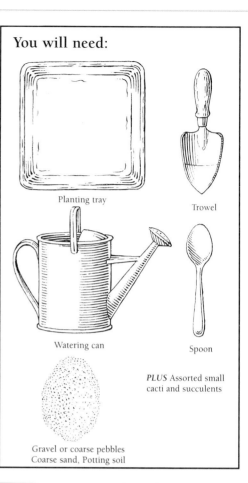

Planting tray

Trowel

Watering can

Spoon

PLUS Assorted small cacti and succulents

Gravel or coarse pebbles
Coarse sand, Potting soil

1. Using a trowel, cover the bottom of the planting tray with a layer of gravel. Then fill it with soil until it is about half full.

Planting tray

Coarse sand

Gravel or coarse pebbles

Potting soil

2. Before taking the plants out of their pots, move them around in the tray until you have found the best arrangement.

3. Using a trowel, dig a hole for each plant. Carefully remove each plant from its pot. Loosen the soil around the roots and plant carefully.

Propeller plant   Haworthia   Easter cactus   Finger-mound cactus   Fish-hook cactus   Thimble cactus

Sand mixture covers the soil.

Fleshy stems store water.

Sharp spines deter plant-eating animals.

Flower in bloom

Be careful not to touch fine hairlike spines.

4. Using a spoon, fill the gaps between each plant with soil. Check that all the plant roots are completely covered.

5. Gently spoon the sand mixture over the potting soil and press it down firmly with the back of a spoon.

6. Your mini desert is now complete. Your plants will need watering about once a week, but be careful not to let the soil get too wet.

43

46 Create a window garden

With your own window garden, you can watch plants closely and see how they grow and flower. Planting a window garden is easy. Before you begin, decide which plants you would like to grow. Try to avoid plants that grow too big. Look for plants with small leaves because they cope better with bright sunlight and sudden gusts of wind. If your window ledge slopes, place some small pieces of wood under the front of the window box to keep it level.

You will need:

Window box and tray

Spray bottle

Trowel

Scissors

Potting soil
Gravel or coarse pebbles

Watering can

PLUS Assorted small flowering plants

Pansy

Impatiens will stay in flower most of the summer.

Marguerite daisy

Gravel or coarse pebbles

Potting soil

Tray collects excess water.

1. Using the trowel, cover the bottom of the window box with a layer of gravel. Then fill the window box with soil until it is about three-quarters full.

2. Decide how you want to arrange the plants. The tallest plants should go at the back, and trailing plants at the front.

44

Bellflower

Impatiens

3. Remember where the plants go, then carefully remove each one from its pot. Gently loosen the roots by pinching at the soil with your fingertips.

4. Dig a hole, and lower a plant into it. Using your knuckles, gently press soil around the plant to make sure it is firmly embedded.

5. Add the rest of the plants until the window box is full. Leave enough room for some growth. Water the garden whenever it appears dry.

Marguerite produces daisy flowers all summer.

If you regularly remove dead flower heads, the plants will flower longer.

Spray the flowers with water to keep them fresh.

Food and drink
Unlike a mini desert (see pages 42–43), your window box will probably need plenty of water. You may want to use some liquid plant food as well.

Bellflower will bloom from summer until early fall.

45

47 Design a butterfly garden

Butterflies are busy animals that are always on the lookout for food. They drink a sugary liquid called nectar, which they collect when they visit sweet-smelling flowers. Try planting some of the nectar-rich flowers below in a window box or, if you have room, grow some in a corner of the garden. Place them in a sunny spot and you will attract an assortment of butterflies in summer and fall.

You will need:

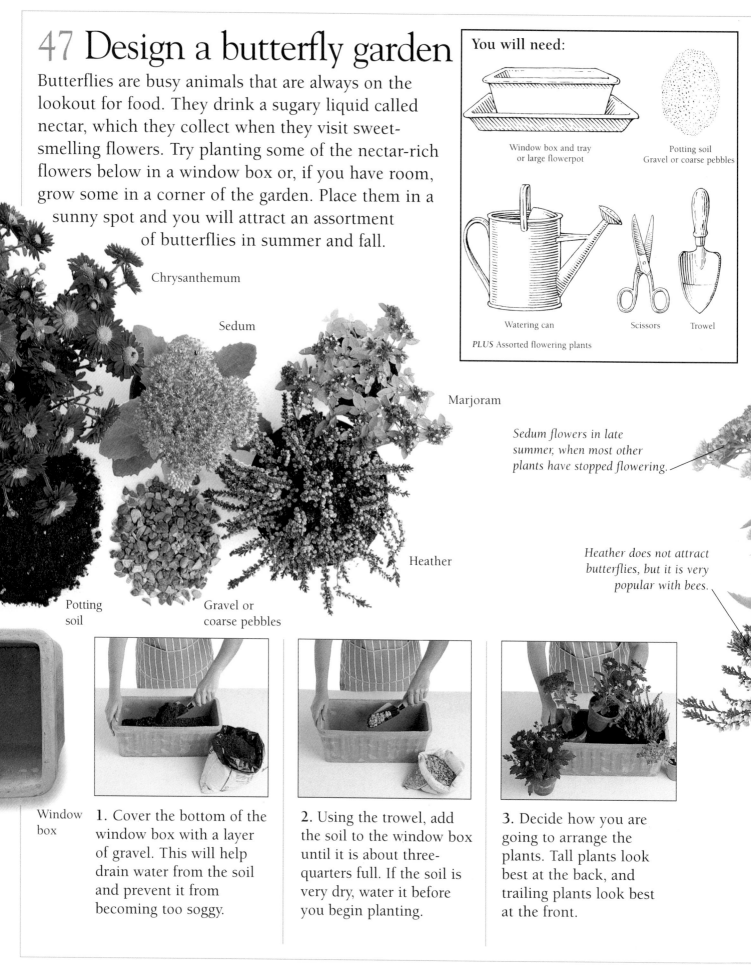

Window box and tray or large flowerpot

Potting soil
Gravel or coarse pebbles

Watering can

Scissors

Trowel

PLUS Assorted flowering plants

Chrysanthemum

Sedum

Marjoram

Heather

Potting soil

Gravel or coarse pebbles

Sedum flowers in late summer, when most other plants have stopped flowering.

Heather does not attract butterflies, but it is very popular with bees.

Window box

1. Cover the bottom of the window box with a layer of gravel. This will help drain water from the soil and prevent it from becoming too soggy.

2. Using the trowel, add the soil to the window box until it is about three-quarters full. If the soil is very dry, water it before you begin planting.

3. Decide how you are going to arrange the plants. Tall plants look best at the back, and trailing plants look best at the front.

4. Turn the first pot upside down and gently ease the plant out. Loosen its roots by pinching at the soil.

5. Dig a hole and then lower the plant into it. Gently pack soil around the plants. Remember to water the flowers regularly.

Blooming attraction

When the plants are in full bloom, their scent and bright colors will attract hungry butterflies and other insects. When you see a butterfly arrive, watch it closely. With luck, you may be able to see its long tongue uncoil and probe into the flowers. A butterfly's tongue works like a drinking straw, sucking up nectar into its mouth.

The flat shape of these daisylike flowers makes an ideal landing platform for a butterfly.

Sweet marjoram is a strong-scented herb that attracts bees and butterflies.

Terracotta window box

48 Grow a salad garden

Here is an easy way to make an instant salad garden – simply grow salad seeds in dampened cotton. You can grow anything that will sprout quickly – cress radish and lettuce seeds will sprout in a few days and be ready to eat in a week. The seeds will sprout all year round, but they must be left in a light spot, such as a sunny windowsill. Salad plants contain substances called vitamins, which are essential to keep your body healthy and strong.

You will need:

Spray bottle

3 glass jars

Pitcher of water

3 saucers

Labels

Sieve

Assorted salad seeds

Cotton

3 clear plastic bags

1. Put the seeds in a sieve and rinse them under cold water. Half-fill the glass jars with water and add seeds. Leave them to stand for about four hours, so they are thoroughly wet.

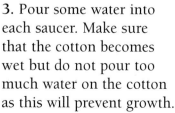

Sprout seeds

Mung bean seeds

2. Place a layer of cotton on each of the saucers. This will give the plants something to anchor their roots into as soon as they start growing.

3. Pour some water into each saucer. Make sure that the cotton becomes wet but do not pour too much water on the cotton as this will prevent growth.

4. Use the sieve to drain the seeds from each jar. Then spread them out evenly on top of the wet cotton so they have enough room for growth.

5. In order for the seeds to germinate they must be kept wet. Spray them every day with plenty of water to make sure they remain damp.

6. Place each saucer inside a plastic bag. This will stop the seeds from drying out. Leave the saucers somewhere warm, such as on a sunny windowsill.

7. In a few days, your seeds will germinate (begin growing). When this happens, take the saucers out of their plastic bags and spray the seedlings to keep them wet. As soon as the seedlings are tall enough, you can harvest them with a pair of scissors.

What happens next?
Your salad garden will not keep growing forever. Even if you keep watering the seedlings, they will eventually start to turn yellow and wither. Seedlings can begin growing without soil, but they need to be in soil to remain healthy.

Two-day-old mung bean seeds

Two-day-old sprout seeds

Mung bean seeds after seven days

Sprout seeds are ready to be harvested.

Check the progress of your salad plants daily.

Sprout seeds after seven days

FLOWERS

FLOWERS ARE THE PLANT PARTS that make seeds. They produce a substance called pollen, which is carried from one flower to another. Every flower has a special shape and color. Some are small and green and spread their pollen with the help of the wind. Others are big and bright and often have a delicious smell. They spread their pollen with the help of insects and other animals.

49 Dissect a flower

From a distance, flowers often look just like clusters of colorful petals. But there is much more to a flower than just its petals. In this experiment you will use a knife to carefully reveal all the parts of a flower that make up the pollen and seeds. Then you can examine them with a magnifying glass.

You will need:

Scissors   Magnifying glass   Craft knife   Tweezers

PLUS Poppy, Buttercup, Tulip, or Lily

👫 *Adult supervision is essential*

Poppy petals

How many petals?
Each plant family has flowers with a characteristic number of petals. Like most plants in the poppy family, this poppy has four petals.

Petal

Receptacle

1. Cut off any green flaps at the back of the flower and then use the knife to slice off the petals where they join the stalk. This will leave you with the center of the flower.

2. Carefully trim away the stalklike stamens and look at them with the magnifying glass. The tips of the stamens are called anthers and they make the flower's pollen. They brush the pollen onto insects or other animals that visit the flower.

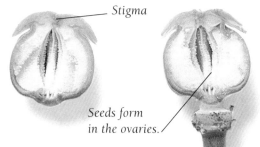

Stigma

Seeds form in the ovaries.

3. You should now be left with the parts of the flower that make the seeds. They collect pollen from the visiting insects and other animals that help scatter the seeds when they are ripe. If you cut open this part of the flower, you may see the seeds inside.

50 Press some flowers

Some flowers bloom for a few hours, while others last for many weeks. In either case, the petals eventually wither away. If you collect some flowers and press them, you can preserve your flowers for as long as you like. Pressing works best with fresh-picked flowers.

You will need:

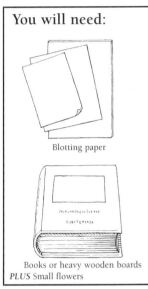

Blotting paper

Books or heavy wooden boards
PLUS Small flowers

1. Put a thick sheet of blotting paper on a book or board. Arrange the flowers on the paper and then cover them with another sheet of paper.

2. Add a heavy weight, such as a pile of books. Leave the flowers for at least a week so they have time to dry. Then carefully lift up the blotting paper and arrange the flowers how you want them. Remember they are fragile, so you must handle them gently.

51 Seeing colors

Flowers get their colors from pigments in their petals. If you dissolve flowers you will see many pigments.

Adult supervision is essential

You will need:

Pestle and mortar   Blotting paper   Pencil

Acetone (nail polish remover)   Glass   Scissors
PLUS Flowers, Stapler

1. Put flowers in a mortar and add 4 tsp (20 ml) of acetone. Grind the mixture with the pestle and put it into a glass. Staple a strip of blotting paper around a pencil and let it hang so it touches the mixture.

Blotting paper soaks up liquid.

Each color you see is a pigment.

2. Leave it for one hour in a well-ventilated room. The acetone will slowly creep up the blotting paper and separate into bands of different colors.

Cut the stems to make the flowers the same length.

Tie the string tight.

Roses have a strong scent.

Baby's breath has small white or pink flowers.

52 Make a dried flower arrangement

Livng flowers do not remain fresh for long, but if you dry flowers you can make them last for a long time. You can press flowers (see page 51), which flattens them while drying, or you can hang them upside down and let them dry, which will preserve the flowers' color and shape.

(see page 51)

You will need:

Scissors

String

PLUS Fresh flowers

String

1. Lay the flowers out on a tabletop and cut their stems so they are all the same length. Arrange the flowers in a bundle and tie them up with some string. Make sure the string is tight because the stems shrink as they dry out. Hang the flowers up somewhere warm and dry.

2. After two weeks, the flowers and leaves will have completely dried out. Cut the string and carefully arrange the flowers in a vase. Place the arrangement where everyone can admire it.

The arrangement takes about two weeks to dry.

53 Preserve flowers

This method of drying flowers is more complicated than the one opposite, but it sometimes gives better results. It uses a substance called silica gel, which absorbs the moisture in flowers. As it absorbs moisture, the gel turns from blue to pink. You can dry it out again by baking it in an oven at a low temperature.

You will need:

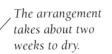

Large glass jar with lid *PLUS* Flowers

Silica gel, available at some craft shops

👯 *Adult supervision is advised*

1. Put a layer of silica gel into a large jar. Then place some flowers upside down in the jar. Make sure that the flowers are well spread out.

Place the flowers upside down.

Silica gel

The color of some flowers may fade.

Tallest stems are placed in the center of the arrangement.

Dried roses often keep their scent and shape.

2. Slowly add more silica gel until the flowers are completely covered. Gently tap the jar to remove any air spaces, then screw the lid onto the jar. Leave the flowers in the jar for at least a week to dry.

Pour the silica gel carefully into the jar.

Leave the flowers for at least a week.

TREES

WOULDN'T IT BE HARD to imagine a world without trees? They are the longest-living plants on dry land, and the biggest. Trees are the most important components of a forest, because they provide food and shelter for all kinds of animals from ants to bears. They also support woodland fungi, which feed on dead wood and fallen leaves, and sometimes living trees.

54 See buds burst

Some trees keep their leaves all year round. Others shed them in the fall, and grow a completely new set in spring. The new leaves actually start to develop in the previous year, but then spend the winter packed tightly as buds. When spring arrives, the buds burst and the new leaves start to grow. You can make buds open early by cutting some twigs and bringing them indoors. Put them in a jar of water and give them plenty of warmth and sunlight.

You will need:

Water
PLUS Twigs (horse chestnuts, poplars, and willows are best)

Jar

Pruning shears

Flower bud

New leaves inside the flower bud begin to unfold.

Leaf scar

Each flower bud is covered with sticky scales that protect it.

Flower bud

New shoot

Scale scar

Soon, bud scales will drop off, leaving a scale scar.

Keep the twigs in clean water.

In early spring, look out for twigs with buds that are beginning to swell. Cut them off, and then put them in water in a well-lit spot such as a sunny windowsill. As the days pass, the leaves inside begin to grow and you will see the bud's outer scales fold back. Eventually, new shoots will break out of the buds, and the leaves will begin to unfold.

55 Discover the age of a tree

By measuring around a tree's trunk, you can get a guide to its age. However, trees grow at different rates. Palm trees and some fast-growing trees, such as conifers, do not follow this guide.

The circumference of a mature tree increases by 1 in (2.5 cm) every year.

1. Hold the tape measure at a height of at least 3 ft (1 m) above the ground and then measure the tree's circumference.

2. Divide the measurement by 1 in (2.5 cm) to discover the tree's approximate age in years.

56 Measure the height of a tree

Guessing the height of a tree can be difficult, because it is hard to compare a tree with anything nearby. Here is an easy way to come up with an accurate answer. To try it out, you will need a friend to help.

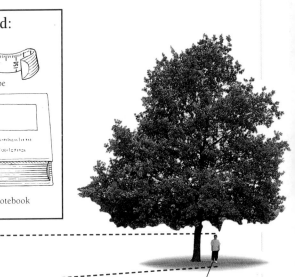

The top lines up with the top of your friend's head.

Pencil mark lines up with friend's feet.

Friend standing under a tree

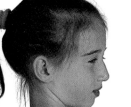

Stick must be held at arm's length.

1. Measure the height of your friend and write it down in your notebook. Then ask him or her to stand at the base of a tree.

2. Hold the stick at arm's length and line up the top of the stick with the top of your friend's head. Then mark the stick where it lines up with your friend's feet.

3. Line the top up with the tree's top and mark the ground line. Multiply the number of times your friend's "height" fits in that space by your friend's real height to calculate the tree's height.

57 Plant a tree

During the fall months, lots of trees drop their leaves and seeds onto the ground. Some seeds germinate (begin growing) a few days after leaving the tree. Others take much longer to grow because they wait until the cold winter weather has passed. If you collect some seeds, you can plant them in pots and watch them grow.

You will need:

3 flowerpots

Pitcher of water

Pen

Plant labels

Trowel

Assorted tree seeds

Watering can

Potting soil
Gravel or
coarse pebbles

1. Put a small amount of gravel into each flowerpot. This will help water drain out. Fill the rest of each pot with soil.

Acorns

Maple seeds

Horse chestnuts

Sweet chestnuts

As the tree grows, its stem becomes much stronger.

2. Plant a different seed in each flowerpot. Push the seeds down in the soil and cover them. Water the soil until it is thoroughly wet.

3. Label each flowerpot with the tree's name. Put the flowerpots somewhere cool and shady (outside is best) and wait for the seeds to start growing.

Growing a maple
Once the tree reaches between 3.9 in (10 cm) and 4.7 in (12 cm), take it out of the flowerpot and plant it in a sunny spot.

58 Make a bark rubbing

Some bark is smooth, but other kinds of bark are rough and full of cracks. If you attach some strong paper to a tree trunk with masking tape and rub it firmly with a wax crayon, you can make a "rubbing" of the bark.

Make a collection of rubbings from different trees and notice how the patterns vary.

Rub firmly over the trunk.

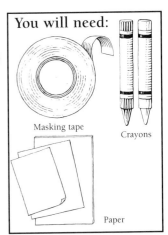

You will need:

Masking tape

Crayons

Paper

59 Make a leaf skeleton

You will need:

Pan of water

PLUS Fallen leaves

Washing soda

When the soft parts of dead leaves rot away, they leave behind a "skeleton" of veins. You can find plenty of leaf skeletons on the ground in the fall. In this experiment you will make them at home by using washing soda, which gently dissolves the soft parts of a leaf.

👭 *Adult supervision is essential*

Veins

Midrib

Stalk

Dead leaf

1. Dissolve some washing soda in a small pan of water. Add the leaves and then gently warm the pan. Do not let it get too hot.

2. Take the pan away from the heat, and leave it for several hours. Remove the leaf skeletons and rinse them thoroughly.

60 Grow mold

Molds do not grow from seeds. Instead, they grow when a spore (dustlike speck) lands on something it can digest. The spore then breaks open, and starts to grow. In this experiment you will see what happens when mold spores land on three slices of bread that are prepared in different ways.

You will need:

Container

Plastic wrap

Disinfectant

Pitcher of water

PLUS 3 slices of bread

1. Put two slices of bread in a container. Leave the third slice out so it will become dry.

2. Try not to let the slices of bread touch. Pour a small amount of disinfectant onto one of the slices. Be careful not to get any on the neighboring slice.

3. Pour enough water on both slices of bread to make them quite damp. But you must be careful not to let any of the water build up in the base of the container.

4. Seal the container with plastic wrap. This will shut in any spores and keep the bread damp. Put all three slices somewhere dark and warm.

5. After three days, look at the result. The damp bread will probably show signs of mold. The dry bread and the disinfected bread have no mold.

Dry bread has no mold.

Moisture and warmth help the mold feed on the bread.

Mold has grown on the damp bread.

The disinfectant kills the spores so no mold can grow.

61 Make a spore print

Mushrooms and toadstools drop tiny spores in the air, enabling fungi to spread. Normally, the wind carries spores far and wide. In this experiment you will use the spores to make a special print. Remember to wash your hands after touching wild mushrooms.

You will need:

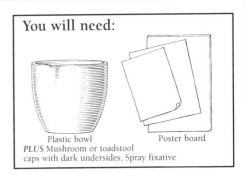

Plastic bowl
Poster board
PLUS Mushroom or toadstool caps with dark undersides, Spray fixative

1. Slice off a mushroom's stalk and put the cap on a piece of poster board. Cover it with a bowl to prevent the spores from being blown away.

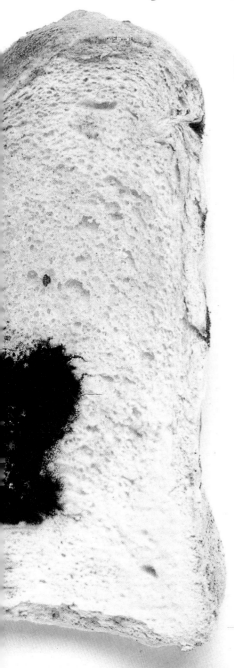

2. The next day, carefully lift off the mushroom's cap. The mushroom's spores will have fallen onto the board and made a print.

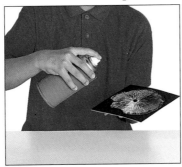

3. To stop the spores from smudging, spray the print with fixative, such as hairspray. When the hairspray is dry, your print will be finished.

Use different colors of poster board.

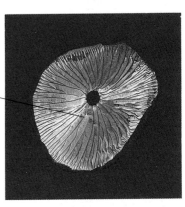

Collect prints of other mushrooms.

The spores fall from underneath the mushroom cap.

62 Make a woodland terrarium

A terrarium is a home in which to keep small animals that live on land. It contains food for them to eat, fresh water for them to drink, and places for them to hide. In this experiment you will find out how to make a terrarium especially suited to small woodland animals. Once you have filled it with dead branches, leaves, and a few beetles and sow bugs, it will resemble a small area of forest floor.

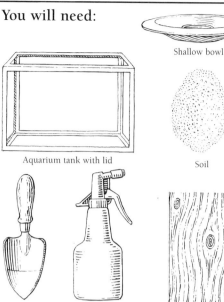

You will need:

Shallow bowl

Aquarium tank with lid

Soil

Trowel

Spray bottle

Small dead branches
Pinecones

PLUS Leaves, Small animals
(Beetles, Sow bugs, Millipedes, and Snails)

Small dead branch

Pinecones

Soil

Leaves

2. Fill the remainder of the tank floor with soil and add some pinecones. Place the bowl in the soil, and fill it with water.

1. Fill one corner of the tank with some dead leaves and wood. This will provide a place for the animals to climb and hide.

3. Add more soil around the bowl to keep it in place. Sprinkle some water over the tank to keep it damp.

4. You can now add your animals. If you have sloping branches in the tank, you will be able to see your animals climb up.

5. If your terrarium contains snails, feed them with fresh, leafy food such as lettuce. Any larger animals you have will also need a supply of food.

Centipedes hunt at night, feeding on animals smaller than themselves.

Centipede

A sow bug has fourteen legs.

Sow bugs

Sow bugs feed on rotting leaves and other parts of dead plants; they can only survive in damp places

House spider

The house spider spins a web shaped like a three-cornered hammock.

The ground beetle has powerful jaws.

Ground beetle

Pinecone

Leave a gap for ventilation.

Use a damp cloth to keep the glass clean.

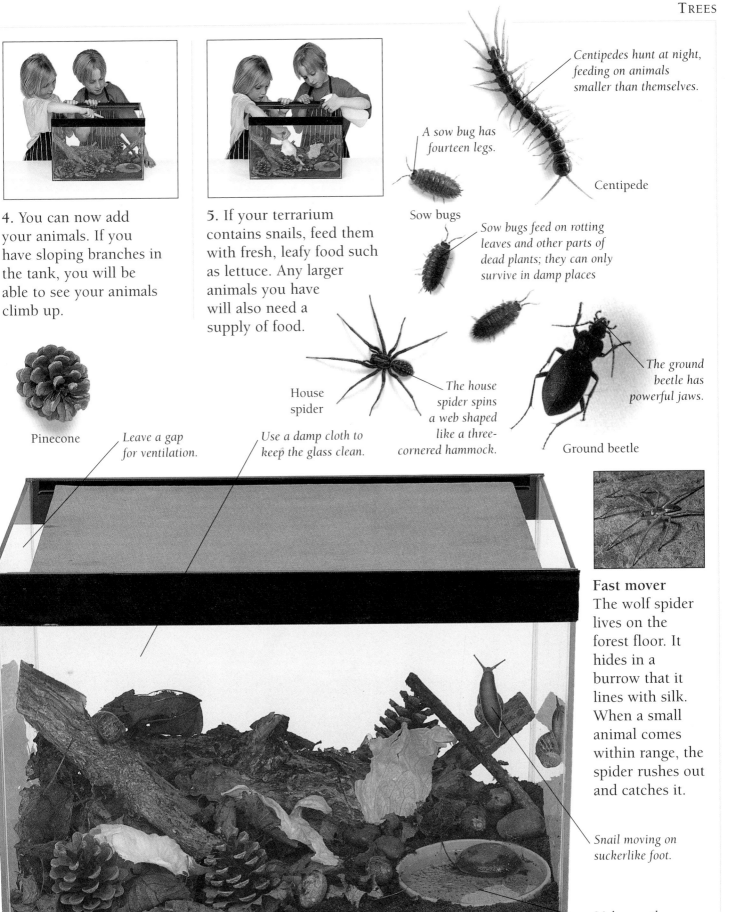

Fast mover
The wolf spider lives on the forest floor. It hides in a burrow that it lines with silk. When a small animal comes within range, the spider rushes out and catches it.

Snail moving on suckerlike foot.

Make sure there is always a fresh supply of water.

SMALL ANIMALS

ABOUT TWO MILLION different kinds of animals have been discovered on Earth. Animals range from tiny, simple creatures to gigantic blue whales. The vast majority of animals are small, however. There are more than one million species of insects and 30,000 different species of spiders alone!

63 Look at insects close up

In spring and summer, trees play host to a huge number of insects. Some eat leaves or sap, while others are hunters that search the tree for prey. Even if you stand close to a tree, few of these insects are easy to see. But with the help of a beater tray, you will be able to see tree-dwelling insects close up.

You will need:

Tacks

Square of white fabric
PLUS Stick

Wooden frame
(see pp. 12–13)

— *Assemble the frame.*

1. The frame used here is the same as for the quadrat on pp. 12–13. Once you have assembled the frame, stretch the fabric over it and use the tacks to fasten it in position.

Watch out for escaping insects.

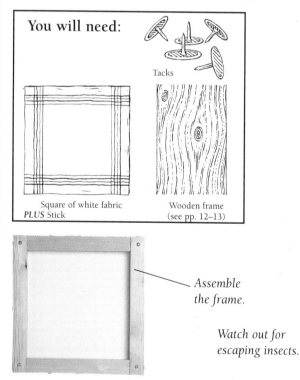

2. Hold the tray under a low, leafy branch and hit the branch several times with a stick (be careful not to break the branch). The insects will lose their grip and tumble onto the tray. If you want, you can repeat the experiment with different trees.

Animal life comes tumbling onto the tray.

64 Make a "pooter"

A pooter is a special device that allows you to pick up fast-moving, small animals without touching or harming them. The pooter works by suction. You suck through one tube and the animals are drawn up through another tube into the jar.

You will need:

Glass jar with lid   Screwdriver   Wire   Tape

Muslin   3 ballpoint pen barrels   Rubber tubing   Rubber band

PLUS Modeling clay

1. Make two holes in the jar's lid with a screwdriver. Cover one end of a pen barrel with muslin. Push the pen barrels through each hole. Seal them both in position with modeling clay.

2. Fit a piece of rubber tubing to the outer end of each pen barrel. Bend the tubing on the barrel without the muslin (you can make it bend by taping wires to it). Add the third barrel to the outer end of the bent tube. Screw on the lid.

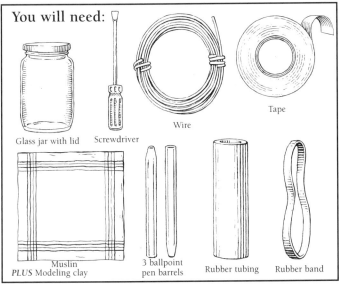

Suction through pipe

Muslin stops insects from going into your mouth.

65 Test a worm's reaction

A worm's tail is extremely sensitive to touch. If a bird touches a worm's tail, the worm will suddenly contract (squeeze up) and pull its whole body underground in order to escape. If you collect an earthworm and lightly touch its tail, you can see what happens.

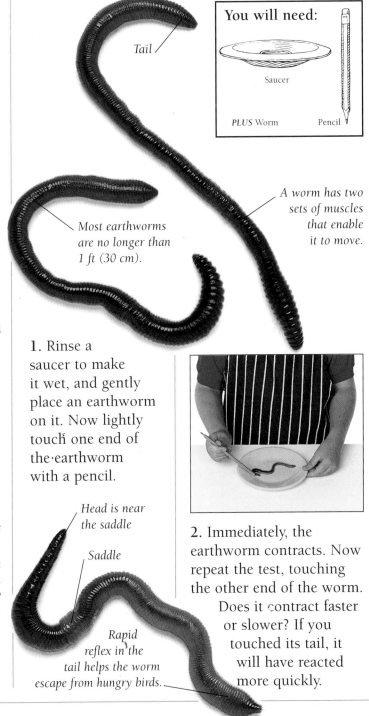

Tail

You will need:

Saucer

PLUS Worm   Pencil

A worm has two sets of muscles that enable it to move.

Most earthworms are no longer than 1 ft (30 cm).

1. Rinse a saucer to make it wet, and gently place an earthworm on it. Now lightly touch one end of the earthworm with a pencil.

Head is near the saddle

Saddle

Rapid reflex in the tail helps the worm escape from hungry birds.

2. Immediately, the earthworm contracts. Now repeat the test, touching the other end of the worm. Does it contract faster or slower? If you touched its tail, it will have reacted more quickly.

66 Build a caterpillar house

Have you ever watched a caterpillar change into a butterfly? If you make your own caterpillar house, you may be lucky enough to see this happen. The best time to collect caterpillars is early spring or summer. Caterpillars are choosy eaters, so make sure you always feed them with the same kind of leaves you found them living on in the wild.

Adult supervision is essential

You will need:

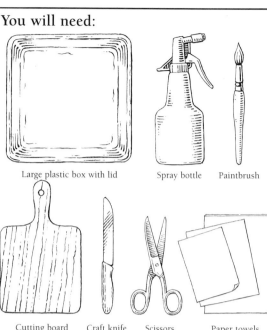

Large plastic box with lid   Spray bottle   Paintbrush

Cutting board   Craft knife   Scissors   Paper towels or tissues

PLUS Caterpillars and leaves for caterpillars to eat, Large piece of muslin, Small twigs

Some caterpillars have tufts or bristles that irritate the skin, so always pick them up with a paintbrush.

Feed your caterpillars with fresh leaves every day.

Twig

A caterpillar changes into a chrysalis (or pupa) when it is fully grown.

5. After a few weeks, you may see the caterpillars change into chrysalises and then into adult butterflies.

Do not prod or disturb the caterpillars because they are very delicate.

Set your butterfly free when it is sunny.

1. Ask an adult to cut around the box's lid so just the rim is left behind. Cut out a piece of muslin big enough to cover the box.

2. Line the box with paper towels and spray it with water until it feels slightly damp. This stops the caterpillars from drying out.

3. Put some twigs in the box and add some leaves. Use the paintbrush to pick up the caterpillars and place them on the leaves.

A caterpillar will molt several times during its life.

4. Put some muslin over the box. Then push the lid down over the muslin to hold it firmly in place. The house is now complete.

67 Make a beehive box

Bumblebees are big, furry bees that start flying early in the year. Female bumblebees lay their eggs in small nests, which they often build underground. Instead of digging a hole, the bumblebee will look for one that has already been made. Nesting sites are often in short supply. If you make the special box shown here, you can help a bumblebee set up home.

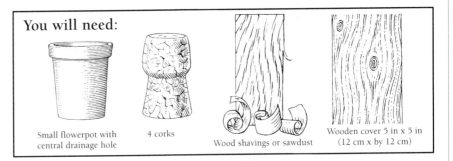

You will need:

Small flowerpot with central drainage hole

4 corks

Wood shavings or sawdust

Wooden cover 5 in x 5 in (12 cm x 12 cm)

Dig a hole in the ground and fill it with a small heap of sawdust or wood shavings. Place the pot upside down, inside the hole, so the drainage hole is level with the ground. Place the wooden cover on the corks, so that a bee is able to crawl underneath.

Build your nest in early spring.

68 Train honeybees

In spring and summer honeybees fly from flower to flower to collect a sugary liquid called nectar. They use the nectar as food, and take it back to their nests. When a bee arrives at the nest, it tells other bees where it can be found. In this experiment, you will train honeybees to come to an artificial flower with a sugary liquid center. As you can see here, lots of bees will soon arrive to feed.

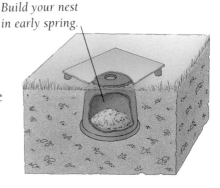

You will need:

Sugar

Pitcher of warm water
PLUS 5 identical bottletops

Poster board

1. Cut out five identical "flowers" from different-colored poster board. Put the bottletops in the centers of the flowers. Now add some sugary liquid to one of the flowers.

Sugary liquid

2. If the weather is warm, a honeybee will soon arrive to investigate the flower and discover the food. After it has flown off, other bees will begin to arrive.

3. Within a short time, lots of bees will be busy feeding at the same flower. They use their long tongues to lap up the sugary water.

Once a bee has found food it fetches other bees.

"Flower" is crowded with bees.

4. Soon the bees are jostling for space. It is quite safe to watch them, but do not disturb them while they are feeding.

69 On the move

Life is full of choices for all animals. They have to choose whether to go in one direction or another, what to eat, and where to hide. The study of animal behavior in nature is known as ethology, and is based on observing the many choices an animal makes. Even simple animals, such as sow bugs, can behave in very complex ways. In this experiment you will see how sow bugs decide between two sets of conditions – dry or moist and light or dark.

Adult supervision is essential

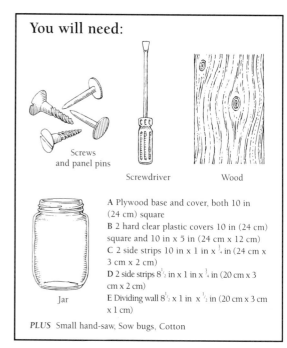

You will need:

Screws and panel pins

Screwdriver

Wood

Jar

A Plywood base and cover, both 10 in (24 cm) square
B 2 hard clear plastic covers 10 in (24 cm) square and 10 in x 5 in (24 cm x 12 cm)
C 2 side strips 10 in x 1 in x ¼ in (24 cm x 3 cm x 2 cm)
D 2 side strips 8½ in x 1 in x ¼ in (20 cm x 3 cm x 2 cm)
E Dividing wall 8½ in x 1 in x ½ in (20 cm x 3 cm x 1 cm)

PLUS Small hand-saw, Sow bugs, Cotton

E

A

C

B

D

1. Screw the side strips (C and D) to the base (A) and cut three openings in the dividing wall (E). Make them large enough for the insects to crawl through. Fix the dividing wall to the base so it splits the space into two equal chambers.

2. Collect some sow bugs (you will find them outside under stones or pieces of wood). Distribute them into each of the chambers. Leave them for at least ten minutes so they are able get used to their new home.

Sow bugs move from one compartment to the other through the small doorway.

Collect sow bugs in a jar and place them in the chamber.

70 Nature's night shift

At night, when it is cool and damp, all sorts of animals come out in search of food. In this experiment you will make an animal shelter from a grapefruit to attract some of these wandering creatures. Leave it overnight, and in the morning you can see what you have caught.

3. To see if sow bugs prefer dry or moist surroundings, place a piece of moistened cotton in one of the compartments and cover the whole box. The following day, see how the bugs are distributed. You will find that most of the sow bugs are in the compartment containing cotton. This is because they prefer moist conditions.

4. To see if sow bugs prefer light or dark conditions, cover one compartment with clear plastic (B) and the other with the wooden lid (A). After four to six hours, see where the bugs are. You will find that most of them have chosen to remain in the covered compartment. This is because sow bugs normally feed after dark, and do not like daylight.

A sow bug is harmless.

You will need:

Cutting board   Knife   Spoon
PLUS Grapefruit

1. Slice the grapefruit in half. Remove the fleshy fruit with the spoon so you are left with only the skin.

2. Place the grapefruit skins outside, hollow side down, on some bare ground. The skins are tough and full of juice. The juice will make the air underneath the fruit moist and attract lots of animals.

Midnight feast
Slugs come out at night, searching for food. This slug has discovered a plum that has fallen from a tree onto the ground.

3. Leave the skins overnight, and then turn them over to see how many different animals have gathered beneath.

Sow bug

Slug

71 Make a spider's web

Many spiders capture flying insects by spinning a silken web. A spider's web looks delicate, but the silk of some webs is stronger than steel wire of the same thickness. A spider builds a sticky spiral out of liquid silk that it squeezes out of its body. As soon as the silk meets the air, it hardens. You can make your own web with some string and pins.

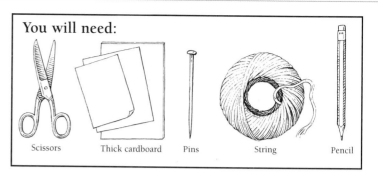

You will need:

Scissors   Thick cardboard   Pins   String   Pencil

1. Cut out a square of cardboard. Each side should be 12 in (30 cm) in length. Mark the center of the cardboard and then draw lines through it.

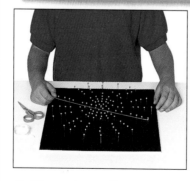

It takes a spider about one hour to spin a web like this.

A real spider's web is made from liquid silk.

5. Your web is now complete. When a spider has finished its web, it waits in the center for an insect to get caught. As soon as a victim lands in the sticky web, the thread shakes, and the spider moves to attack.

2. Place a pin at the top of each line so you create a large circle. Repeat with the remaining pins so you make smaller circles. Continue until you reach the center of the cardboard.

3. Tie a piece of string from each outer pin to its opposite, crossing the center, all the way around the circle, creating lines like the spokes of a wheel.

4. Then carefully weave a spiral outward from the center of the web until you reach the edge. A real spider would spiral back into the center.

Recycled silk
Spiders often have to repair their webs. When a web is damaged, a spider eats it, and then weaves a new one. In this way, it recycles its silk.

72 Make a moth trap

Moths are often attracted to bright lights, which is why they sometimes flutter into lit rooms through open windows after dark. Moths have short wings and stubby bodies. If you want to get a closer look at some night-flying moths, try making the simple moth trap shown here.

You will need:

Shoe box   Funnel   Sharp knife   Lamp

Male oak eggar
Male moths often have feathery antennae (feelers).

Adult supervision is advised

1. Carefully cut through the funnel with a sharp knife, so that a hole at least 1 in (2.5 cm) wide is left at the narrow end.

Front wing

Clever disguise
The lappet moth folds its wings over its body to resemble dead leaves.

Hind wing

2. Cut a hole in the top of the shoe box, wider than the narrow end of the funnel. The funnel should sit upright in the hole.

Abdomen

Female lobster moth
This moth's caterpillar has a tail like a lobster's.

Bright light attracts moths.

4. Put the funnel in position and plug in the lamp. Lower the lamp so that it is about 8 in (20 cm) above the funnel and switch it on. Leave it for one or two hours. Then pull the box away from the lamp and carefully lift the lid. Your moths should be sitting inside.

If you make the hole in the funnel and the shoe box wider, you will trap larger moths.

3. After dark, put the shoe box outside. Keep it away from bright lights such as street lamps so the moths are not distracted.

73 Animal tracks

Many wild animals are naturally shy, and will quickly run away if they hear you coming. But if you look carefully on the ground, you can sometimes find the tracks that these animals leave behind. The shape of the tracks and the way they fit together can often tell you what animal has made them. Tracks form best on soft ground or snow. Use the special track tray shown here, and you will see tracks formed in sand.

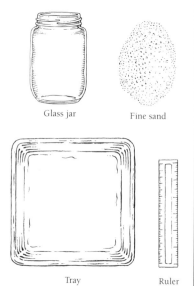

You will need:

Glass jar   Fine sand

Tray   Ruler

Sand with very fine grains produces the clearest results.

1. Pour the sand into the tray or directly onto the ground. Make it slightly damp with a little water to ensure that it does not move around after an animal has stepped on it.

2. Drag the ruler across the sand to give it a smooth, flat surface. If you are using a tray, place it outside in the ground so that it is level with the soil around it.

Tiger feet
These tracks were made by a tiger walking across soft mud. Domestic cat tracks look almost exactly the same, but smaller.

3. First thing in the morning, check the sand for tracks. If any are there, see if you can figure out which animal they belong to. Small, round paw prints without claw marks are often made by cats. Bigger prints with claw marks are made by raccoons, badgers, and other nocturnal animals. If the tracks are evenly spaced, the animal that made them was probaby walking or running. If they are in pairs, it was hopping.

74 Make a plaster cast

In the wild, tracks do not last for long. They disappear as the wind blows, or as rain washes across the soil. But with the help of some quick-setting plaster of paris, you can keep a permanent collection of any tracks that you find. This method works best on damp sand and mud. It does not work in snow, because the liquid plaster is warm before it becomes solid, and it will melt the tracks.

You will need:

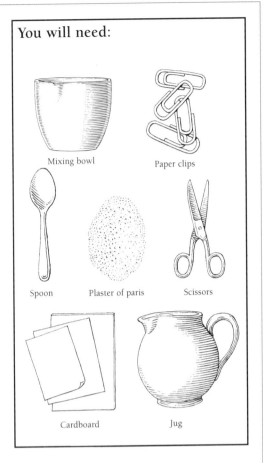

Mixing bowl

Paper clips

Spoon

Plaster of paris

Scissors

Cardboard

Jug

1. Once you have located some tracks, gently brush away any leaves or twigs around them. Pick out any pieces of mud that have fallen into the tracks so that you have a clean print.

2. Use the paper clips to fasten a strip of cardboard into a ring slightly bigger than the tracks. Position the ring around the tracks, and then press it gently into the soil about ½ in (1 cm) deep. Make sure there are no gaps around the bottom of the ring through which the liquid plaster could flow out.

3. Mix up some plaster, adding water a little bit at a time until it is thick, but runny. Pour the liquid mixture into the cardboard ring and smooth the surface. Wait for it to set, which will take about an hour. When the plaster is firm to the touch, lift it up, with the cardboard ring still attached to it.

Raised casts of deer tracks

4. Let the plaster dry out for at least a day. Once it is dry, remove the cardboard. The tracks stick out of the plaster, but otherwise they are just like the ones in the ground. Collect plaster casts of different tracks and compare them.

75 Track snails

When studying wild animals, it is useful to find out where they go. Marking animals can show how far they travel, and keep track of how many there are. In this experiment you will do some wildlife tracking in your own garden or backyard.

You will need:

Flowerpot

Paintbrush

Enamel paint
PLUS Garden snails

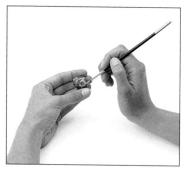

1. Pick up each snail and tap it to make it pull in its body. Using the paintbrush, mark a number on the shell, taking care not to get any paint on the snail's body.

Number identifies each snail.

2. Put the snails in the flowerpot and then see where you find them on the following days. What is the farthest distance that they travel from their home?

A large clay flowerpot makes an ideal home for snails.

Snails rest in damp places.

76 Raise fruit flies

Insects live on an amazing variety of different foods. Some feed on plants, some chew their way through wool, some even drink blood! In this experiment you can raise tiny flies that feed on fruit. In summer, fruit flies wander through the air, searching for a suitable place to lay their eggs.

You will need:

Square piece of cloth

Rubber band

Knife

Glass jar
PLUS Cutting board, Banana

Adult supervision is advised

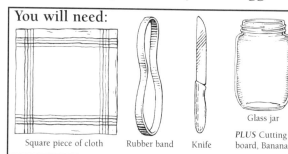

1. Choose a banana that is thoroughly ripe. The smell of the banana will attract female fruit flies that are ready to lay eggs.

Cover the bananas after a few days.

Leave the bananas in a warm and bright place.

DAY 2

72

2. Cut the banana into several pieces that are each 1 in (2.5 cm) long. There is no need to peel the banana first.

3. Put the pieces of banana in the jar. Leave it uncovered and put it in a warm and bright place until the banana begins to turn black.

4. Fasten the fabric over the jar with the rubber band. Keep the jar in a warm and bright place and check it every day for any signs of change.

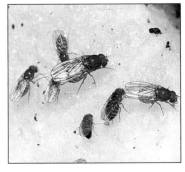

Fruit feast
The fruit flies shown on this banana are magnified. However, you will need good eyesight to spot them. They are only about 1/10 in (3 mm) long!

Fruit flies hatch in only ten days.

Fabric over the jar will stop the fruit flies from escaping.

DAY 10

5. If the banana has been visited by fruit flies, the eggs will soon hatch. If it is warm, they will turn into flies in about ten days.

BIRDS

MOST BIRDS ARE SHY ANIMALS. They have lots of enemies and are always on the lookout for signs of danger. Birdwatching can be a fascinating hobby, but you must be very quiet. A sudden movement or a loud noise will scare a bird away. You can study birds in the wild, or encourage them to nest in your own garden or backyard.

77 Outdoor birdwatching

If you go birdwatching, you must take along two pieces of essential equipment – a pair of binoculars and a notebook. Binoculars allow you to see birds clearly without having to get too close, and with a notebook, you can record what you see. Some birdwatchers take along a field guide, which is a book that shows what each bird looks like. When you go birdwatching, see how many different birds you can spot in a day.

You will need:

Pencil   Notebook   Crayons

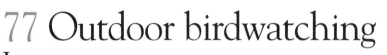

Use your notebook to sketch what you see.

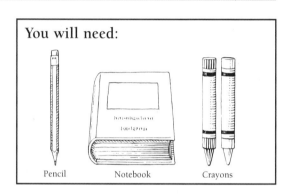

Eyepiece lens

Binoculars should be light and have a good magnification.

Keeping notes
You can make notes about the birds you see, or better yet, draw them and color them in. A quick drawing is often a good way to remember an unusual feature, such as the shape of a bird's wing, or the way it flies.

Using binoculars
The best birdwatching binoculars magnify by about eight or ten times. Some binoculars magnify more, but they are heavy, and difficult to use.

78 Make a blind

If you want to spend the whole afternoon birdwatching and study birds more carefully, why not make a blind? Once inside a blind, you are completely camouflaged. You will be able to take a close look at the daily activities of birds without them being aware of your presence. In your blind you can use your binoculars and take detailed notes about all the birds you see. You can look at the shape and color of birds, and watch the way they live. The blind is built just like a tent. You will need an adult to help you.

Adult help is essential

You will need:

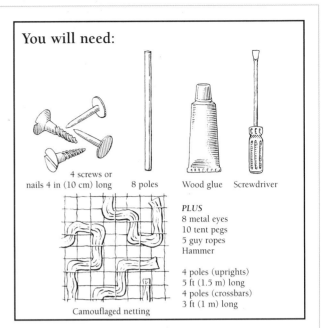

4 screws or nails 4 in (10 cm) long   8 poles   Wood glue   Screwdriver

PLUS
8 metal eyes
10 tent pegs
5 guy ropes
Hammer

4 poles (uprights)
5 ft (1.5 m) long
4 poles (crossbars)
3 ft (1 m) long

Camouflaged netting

1. Hammer a nail to the top of each upright, leaving 2 in (5 cm) protruding. Screw the eyes to the ends of the crossbars and use some glue for extra strength.

3. Tie a guy rope around the top of each upright. Make sure the ropes are at a 45° angle to the frame and use tent pegs to anchor each on to the ground.

5. Peg down three sides of the netting. Decide on the best side for entry to the blind. Cover the blind with some leaves to complete the camouflage.

Camouflaged netting

2. Lift up the poles and crossbars so they are upright. Now check that the frame is standing in a square.

4. Check that each of the guy ropes is tightly anchored to the ground. Throw the camouflage netting over the frame and guy ropes.

6. Once you are inside the blind, clear a hole on each side to give you a good all-around view. You are now ready to do some interesting birdwatching.

Wooden poles

79 Make a nest box

Finding a home can be a difficult task for a small bird. The nest must not only be sheltered from wind and rain, it must also be beyond the reach of cats and other predators. You can encourage birds to breed in your yard by making a wooden nest box. The finished box is designed to last for many years, but will need cleaning out every fall after the family of birds has left.

🖐 *Adult supervision is essential*

You will need:

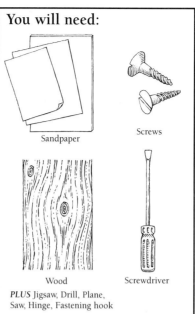

Sandpaper   Screws

Wood   Screwdriver

PLUS Jigsaw, Drill, Plane, Saw, Hinge, Fastening hook

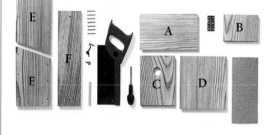

Wood ¼ in (2 cm) thick:
A Back panel 10 in x 6 in (25 cm x 15 cm)
B Floor 4 ½ in x 6 in (11 cm x 15 cm)
C Front panel 8 in x 6 in (20 cm x 15 cm)
D Roof 8 in x 9 in (20 cm x 22 cm)
E 2 side panels 6 in (15 cm) wide, rear height 10 in (25 cm), front height 8 in (20 cm)
F Fixing panel 16 in x 4 in (40 cm x 10 cm)

1. Make an entrance hole 1⅛ in (29 mm) in diameter in the front panel (C). Sand any rough bits smooth. In the other panels, drill pilot holes for the screws, as shown below far left.

2. Plane the top of the back and front panels (A and C) so the roof can lie flat on top of them. Plane the back of the roof (D) so that it fits snugly against the fixing panel (F) when it is shut.

3. First screw the fixing panel (F) to the back panel (A). Next screw on the side panels (E), the floor (B), and the front (C). Finally, attach the roof (D) by the hinge.

4. Fit the hook to the back of the box. Hang the box at least 6½ ft (2 m) above the ground in a shaded place.

80 Examine an old nest

You should never disturb a nest while its owners are still raising a family. But after the breeding season is over, usually by midsummer, the birds will have flown away, and you can safely collect an old nest to see how it is put together. Make absolutely sure it is no longer in use – birds sometimes raise more than one family a year. Wash your hands when you have finished the experiment.

🌳 *Protect the natural world*

You will need:

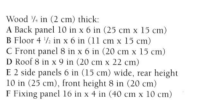

Glue   Labels   Cardboard

Pencil   Magnifying glass   Tweezers

PLUS Old bird's nest

1. Look for an old nest. The most likely place to find one is in a hedge or tree. When you have found an empty one, carefully ease it away from its site. You may need to cut through small twigs with shears, if the nest has been built around them.

2. Begin your investigation by looking inside the nest. It may still contain food remains and broken shells, giving some clues about the birds who lived in it. You may find types of building material vary according to location.

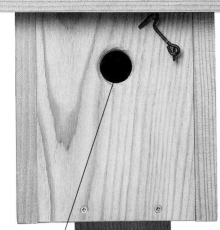

Small hole
keeps out
predators.

Positioning your nest box
The box is more likely to be used
if it is near some leafy branches that
can be used as a lookout. But a new
owner may not come at once. Birds
take time to decide on a new nest.

81 Make an egg-viewing box

This egg viewer works like an X-ray
machine to show you an egg's yolk.

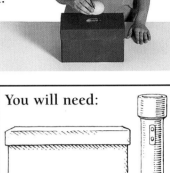

Make hole
smaller
than egg.

1. Cut an oval hole in the lid
of the box. Put the flashlight
inside, so that it is shining upward.

2. Place the egg over the hole
so that it is lit from underneath.
If the egg is fertilized, a darker
patch will be visible; this is the
outline of the developing chick.

You will need:

Shoebox   Flashlight

PLUS Egg

This way of looking at eggs is
often used to separate fertilized
from unfertilized eggs.

For the best results use
the viewer in a dark room.

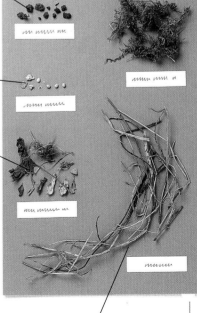

Different nests may
be made of different
building materials.

Tweezers make
it easy to pick
up delicate objects.

Mud from
nest lining

Moss

Broken
eggshells

Leaves

Nest lining is
made of mud.

3. Using the
tweezers, carefully
tease apart the nest.
Separate the different
building materials.
Glue a sample of each
onto a piece of
cardboard and label it.

Grass

82 Bird food

In fall, many birds fly off to faraway places where the weather is warm and where they can find plenty of food. Other birds stay behind. For these birds food is scarce. Here you will find out how to make some simple bird feeders that will help them survive the harsh winter months. Feeding the birds will also give you a chance to watch them. If you are lucky, the same birds will keep returning.

👪 *Adult supervision is advised*

Bird pudding is easy to make and is an ideal way to use up your kitchen ledftovers.

Great tit

You will need:

String

Yogurt or plastic container

Bowl

Small saucepan

Wooden spoon

Scissors

Needle

PLUS Kitchen scraps, birdseed, nuts, lard, pinecone, small twig, fresh coconut, and fine mesh bag

Lard

Yogurt container

Small twig

String

Peanuts in their shells and pecans

Grated cheese

Leftover cooked vegetables

Cooked rice

Mixed nuts

Oats

Birdseed

Brown breadcrumbs

Pinecone

1. To make bird pudding mix all the kitchen scraps together in a bowl. Ask an adult to warm up the lard until it has completely melted.

2. Carefully pour the melted lard into a bowl (remember that it is very hot!). Stir the mixture well with a wooden spoon.

3. Spoon the mixture into the yogurt container, and push a small twig into the middle. Leave the pudding to set in a cool place for an hour.

4. When the pudding has set, squeeze the sides of the container. Ease the pudding out by pulling the twig. Roll the pudding in birdseed, tie string around the twig.

Make a pinecone perch
Press the pudding mixture between the scales of a pinecone. Tie some string to the pointed end of the pinecone so you can hang it upside down.

Make a peanut necklace
Tie a knot in the end of a piece of string. Then use a darning needle to push the string through the soft husk that surrounds the nuts.

Fresh coconut is a favorite of many birds.

Coconut feeder
Coconuts make an excellent winter food for birds. When the coconut flesh is all eaten, fill the shell with bird pudding.

Pinecone perch
A pinecone gives small birds something to perch on while they are feeding. But birds have to work hard in order to reach all the food.

Bird pudding between the scales

You can watch the birds sway as they feed on the pinecone.

Peanuts are an excellent bird food in winter because they are high in fat and protein.

Fine mesh bag

Bag of nuts
You can easily make this feeder. Simply add some nuts to a fine mesh bag. Make sure that the bag is beyond the reach of squirrels and other small mammals.

Peanut necklace
Birds quickly learn to peck the husks off peanuts. Never feed birds with salted nuts because these can make them sick.

Woodpeckers and other birds can break open the shells.

Knot in string

Blue tit

83 Make a feather collection

Throughout their lives, birds gradually shed their feathers and replace them with new ones. This is called molting, and it helps keep their plumage (body and wing feathers) in peak condition. You can find feathers under trees in parks and other places where birds like to perch. Here, you will see how to make special stands to display them.

👥 *Adult supervision is advised*

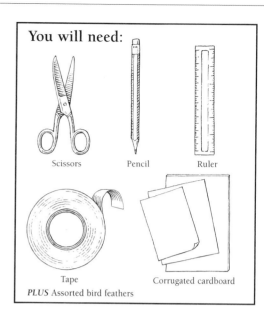
1. If the feathers you find are dusty, clean them in soapy water. When the feathers are dry, pull them through your fingers to arrange them neatly. Spread them on a tabletop and choose your favorite ones to make the collection.

Feather types
A bird's feathers come in many beautiful colors and shapes. They are very light, making it easy for birds to stay in the air.

2. To make the display stands, cut out equal-sized strips of corrugated cardboard. Use the tape to fasten the strips together in pairs.

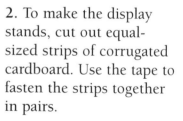

3. Each feather has a stiff central shaft, called a quill. Slide the quill into a hole in the cardboard. This will hold the feather in the stand.

4. When your stand is finished, try putting it against a window. You will be able to see that each feather is made of tiny threads that are attached to the quill.

Woodpigeon feather

Rook feather

Pheasant feather

Blue macaw feather

White goose feather

Quill

Feathers tall and small
The long feathers in the stand are the ones a bird uses to fly. The small feathers cover a bird's body and help keep it warm and dry.

5. These feathers come from an assortment of birds. When your collection is ready, see if your friends can guess which birds the feathers belong to and where on a bird's body they would be found.

81

84 Examine owl pellets

When owls catch small animals, they swallow them whole. Later on, they cough up "pellets", containing the parts they cannot digest. If you look in old barns or under fenceposts, you may be able to find some owl pellets yourself and discover what an owl has been eating.

Owl pellet is hard and dry.

1. Half-fill the glass jar with water and add a few drops of dishwashing liquid. Drop in the pellet, screw the lid on tightly, and shake the jar well.

2. Leave the jar to stand for five minutes and then pour the contents into a sieve. Use the tweezers to pick out skulls, bones, and teeth from the debris.

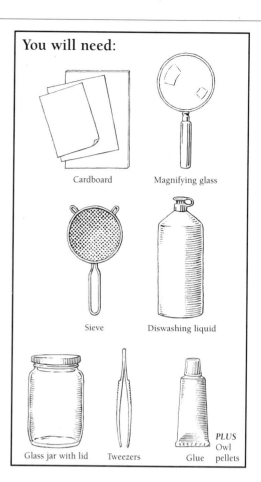

You will need:

Cardboard Magnifying glass

Sieve Diswashing liquid

Glass jar with lid Tweezers Glue

PLUS Owl pellets

85 Design a nature diary

There are so many things to observe in the natural world that it is easy to forget what you have seen. A good way to remember is to keep a nature diary. This kind of diary does not always have to be written in words. You can make drawings of things that you have seen, and you can even include some of the things that you have found. If you keep a diary for a whole year, you can see how plant and animal life changes as one season follows another.

Press some leaves and glue them in your diary.

Seedling growing in a jar

You will need:

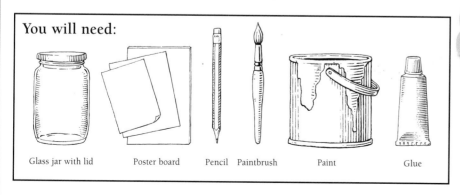

Glass jar with lid Poster board Pencil Paintbrush Paint Glue

Matted fur

Fur and bones are matted together.

Complete pellet

Vole teeth

Shoulder blades

Vole skulls

Front limbs   Hip bones

Leg bones

Jaws

Curved ribs

Incisors

Vertebrae from a starling's backbone

Starling skull

Beak

Wishbone

Legs

Ribs

Claw   Leg bones

Flight feathers

Body feathers

3. Rinse the parts you have collected and then let them dry. The bones belong to mice, voles, and other small mammals. If you look at the skulls with a magnifying glass, you will be able to see their different shapes. To keep your collection, glue the parts to a piece of cardboard.

Examine the bones with a magnifying glass

Feathers found in the woods

Draw any new birds that you may see and label any special colors or markings.

Primrose

THE HUMAN BODY

TO MOST PEOPLE, humans and animals seem very different. Humans consider themelves more intelligent than animals and can do lots of things that animals can't. But despite these differences, humans are in fact animals. Just like other animals, we need water, food, and oxygen to survive, and we use our senses to find out about the outside world and our muscles to react to it.

86 Blood flow and gravity

Blood flows through every part of your body, from your head to your toes. It is pushed by your heart, which pumps hard to counteract the pull of gravity. In this experiment you will see what happens if you make your heart work even harder.

Darker hand

Paler hand

Feeling faint
If you get up suddenly, you may sometimes feel slightly dizzy. This happens because your brain runs short of blood until your heart adjusts to your new position.

Blood drains from the hand that is higher.

1. Hold one of your arms up as high as you can, and let the other hang down. Stay like this for at least a minute.

Blood collects in the hand that is lower.

2. Compare both hands. You should find that the higher hand is paler than the lower hand. The difference in color is caused by gravity. It drains blood out of the higher hand, but holds it back in the lower hand.

87 Watch a tooth disintegrate

The strongest substance in your body is tooth enamel. Enamel is very tough, but it cannot cope with a chemical attack. See what happens when you put a tooth in a glass of soda. Leave it for 24 hours and then examine it. Soda contains acids. Just like food acids, these chemicals attack teeth and break down their tough outer surfaces.

You will need:

Glass of soda
PLUS A tooth

Soda drinks attack the tooth, causing decay.

88 See how fast you grow

As you get older, your body gets bigger and changes shape. But growth is not a smooth process. Newborn babies grow very quickly until they are two years old, then growth slows down. In your early teenage years, growth speeds up again. By the age of 18, most people have reached their adult height.

You will need:

Paint

Paper

Ruler

Pencil

Notebook

PLUS A few friends

You can see how fast you and your friends are growing by marking your heights on a chart. If you are growing very quickly, you should be able to see the difference in just a few months.

Stand up straight as you are measured.

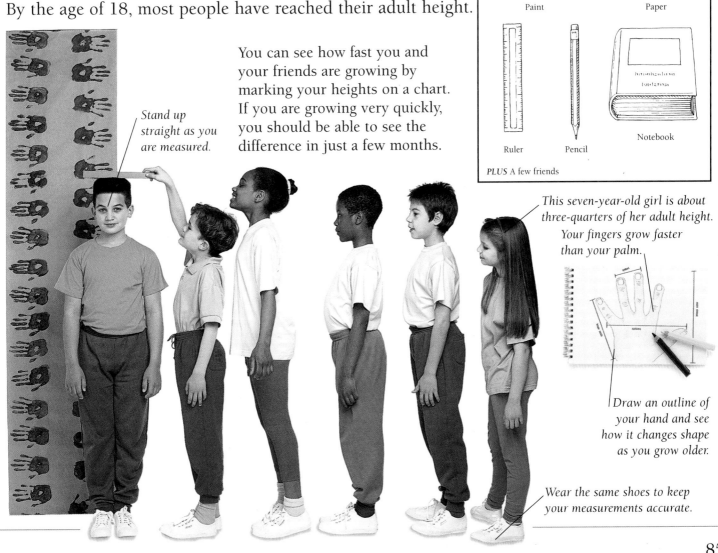

This seven-year-old girl is about three-quarters of her adult height. Your fingers grow faster than your palm.

Draw an outline of your hand and see how it changes shape as you grow older.

Wear the same shoes to keep your measurements accurate.

89 See your pulse rate

Every time your heart beats, it sends a wave of pressure through your blood. This wave is called a pulse. You can feel your pulse with your fingertips where an artery carries blood, such as on the

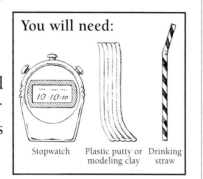
inside of your wrist. The rate of your pulse gives a rough guide to the general health of your heart and body. In this experiment you will make your pulse visible with the aid of a simple pulse meter made from a piece of putty and a drinking straw.

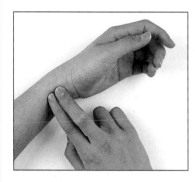

1. Hold out one of your hands with the inside of your wrist facing toward you. Use your fingertips to feel for the pulse in your wrist, below your thumb.

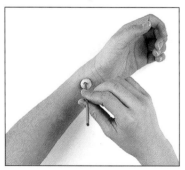

2. Put a blob of putty over the place where you can feel your pulse most strongly. Press a straw into the putty so that it sticks upright from your wrist.

The pulse rate of a ten-year-old is around 80–90 beats per minute.

3. Lie the back of your wrist on a table. If the putty is in the right place, the straw will rock slightly every time a pulse passes. You can measure your pulse rate by counting the number of times the straw moves in one minute. Try this first after you have been resting, and then again after exercising. How much does your pulse rate change? The rate will be slower after resting and faster after exercise.

90 See your skin change color

Most people's skin adapts to changing light conditions. If it is exposed to bright sunshine, it turns darker, which helps shield it against the harmful rays of the Sun. But what happens if skin is kept in the dark? By covering a small patch of skin with a bandage, you can find out. If the bandage becomes dirty, replace it with a new one on the same patch of skin.

1. Wrap the bandage around one of your fingers. Leave it on for several days, and expose the rest of your hand to plenty of light during this time.

2. When you are ready, take the bandage off and look underneath. Can you see any difference in the skin color? Does the patch of skin feel any different if you touch it?

Skin and moisture
After you have worn a bandage for several days, you may notice that the skin under it has become wrinkly. This happens because skin normally gives off moisture, or sweat. If sweat cannot evaporate, it soaks the outer part of the skin, producing wrinkles.

91 Collect fingerprints

The skin on your fingertips is covered with ridges. These form swirling patterns that are known as fingerprints. With the help of some friends, you can collect different sets of fingerprints and carry out some detective work to track down a mystery suspect!

👥 *Adult supervision is advised*

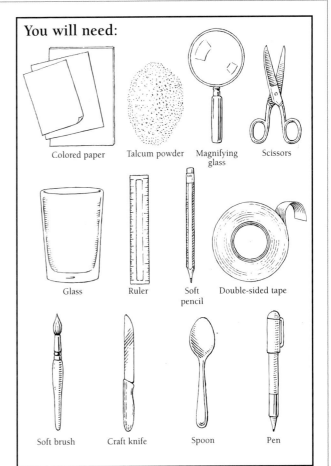

You will need:

Colored paper   Talcum powder   Magnifying glass   Scissors

Glass   Ruler   Soft pencil   Double-sided tape

Soft brush   Craft knife   Spoon   Pen

1. Mark out ten boxes on a piece of paper. Cut out ten small squares of double-sided tape and stick a square in each box.

2. On another piece of paper, rub the soft pencil against paper to make a patch of powder. Ask a friend to dab his or her finger on the patch.

3. Press the finger on a square of the double-sided tape. Repeat with each finger. Collect sets of prints from other friends.

4. While you are not looking, ask one of your friends to pick up the glass.

5. Scrape off some pencil lead with the knife. Using the spoon, mix the lead with a teaspoon of talcum powder.

Dark paper makes fingerprints easy to see.

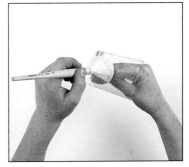

6. Put one hand inside the glass, and dust the outside with the mixture. The fingerprints should now become visible.

7. Use your fingerprint collection and the magnifying glass to find out which friend picked up the glass. Can you tell which hand they used?

92 Lose your balance

Balance is an ability that most of us take for granted. It tells you which way is up, and also whether you are speeding up or slowing down. Unlike other senses, balance works by collecting clues from many parts of the body. Follow the four steps here in your bare feet and you will find out what happens when some of those clues are taken away.

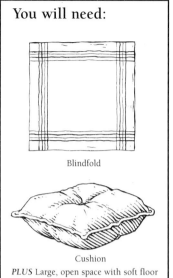

You will need:

Blindfold

Cushion

PLUS Large, open space with soft floor

Adult supervision is advised

Outstretched arms adjust your gravity.

Sensors on the soles of your feet detect pressure as your body tilts and sways.

Be sure an adult is nearby to catch you if you fall.

1. Stand on the cushion with your arms held out. The cushion separates your feet from the ground, making it slightly more difficult for you to stand upright.

2. Now stand on one leg. Your brain has only half the information necessary to keep you balanced, and you will start to wobble.

3. Ask an adult to blindfold you. Without clues from your eyes to report the position of your head in relation to its surroundings, your brain has a much harder time telling if you are upright.

4. Now hold your arms by your sides. This makes it even more difficult to stay upright because moving your arms also helps you balance. Within a few seconds, you will probably fall over! Try this part of the experiment again, but without the blindfold. Being able to see will help you stay up longer.

Stand on one foot.

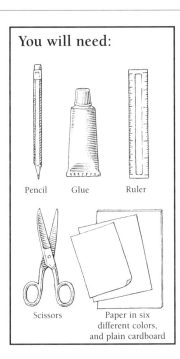
93 Test your reactions

If you accidentally touch something hot, your hand will pull away before you even have time to think. This is called a reflex, and it is a built-in response that protects you from danger. Reactions are like reflexes, but they have to be learned. The more you use them, the faster they get. See how your reactions improve by testing them on a colored scale.

Squares of colored paper

Hold the strip by its upper tip.

Colored scale makes it easy to measure your reactions.

1. Cut the colored paper into equal-sized squares. Glue them to a strip of cardboard, putting the same sequence of colors on both sides.

2. Ask a friend to hold the strip by the upper tip. Place your thumb and index finger 1 in (2.5 cm) below the strip, ready to catch it as soon as it begins to fall. Ask your friend to drop the card without any warning. Catch it by closing your thumb and index finger as fast as you can. Where are you are holding it?

3. The closer to the bottom you catch the strip, the quicker your reactions. You should be able to improve your time with practice, but may reach a stage (color) that you cannot get past.

94 Trick your eyes

Your eyes receive more information than any other sense organ. When you look at anything, your eyes send signals to your brain. Your brain then puts the signals together and gives you a picture of the outside world. Normally your eyes and brain give you an exact picture of what you see. But sometimes this does not happen. Try out these two experiments to reveal your blind spot and see how the brain sometimes misunderstands what it sees.

Blind spot
This experiment proves that your eyes actually have a "blind spot." This means that your brain does not always see everything in front of you. You'll also find out that your brain sometimes misunderstands what it sees.

You will need:

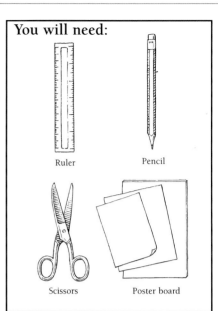

Ruler   Pencil

Scissors   Poster board

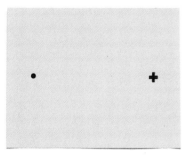

1. Take a piece of poster board and mark a cross and a dot on it. Make sure the dot and cross are at least 4 in (10 cm) apart.

Eye teaser
Draw two lines the same length and add some arrows as shown. Do both lines look the same length? The lower line looks longer. This is because the direction of the arrows confuses the brain into thinking it is longer, even though it isn't.

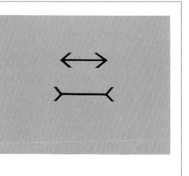

Keep your left eye on the cross.

Pull the board slowly away.

2. Hold up the board, at arm's length. Make sure that the marked cross is on the right-hand side of the board. Cover your right eye and look at the cross with your left eye.

3. Move the board slowly away, keeping your left eye on the cross. At a certain distance, the dot will completely disappear!

95 Test your taste threshold

How strong does the taste of something have to be before you are able to detect that it is there? In this experiment you will be able to discover how good your sense of taste is by testing your ability to taste salt. All you have to do is make up six different strengths of salty water. Sip a little of each mixture, until the taste of salt becomes noticeable.

You will need:

Salt

Pitcher of water

Food coloring

Spoon

6 glasses

1. Put 2 tbs (1 oz/30 g) of salt into 1 quart (liter) of water. Add a drop of food coloring to make the dilution visible. Stir it well so that all the salt dissolves.

2. Fill the first glass with the solution. Then pour out some of the solution from the pitcher until it is only half full. Top it up with water so that the salt solution is halved.

4. Take a sip of the weakest solution to see if you can taste the salt. If not, move to the next glass. As soon as you taste salt, you have reached your threshold level.

Food coloring makes the dilution visible.

Strongest solution of salt

3. Put the remaining glasses in a line and fill the second glass with the diluted solution. Repeat step two, so the salt content is again reduced. Keep halving the strength of salty water for each additional glass.

Begin the experiment with the weakest solution of salt.

96 Test your blind spot

If you have tried to do the experiment on page 90, you have discovered that each of your eyes has a small "blind spot." But when you look around, there are no gaps in your vision. This is because our eyes are constantly flicking about, so any gap rarely stays in the same place for long. This experiment proves that even when you focus on an object and keep your eyes completely still, your brain will fill in any gaps by guessing the missing details.

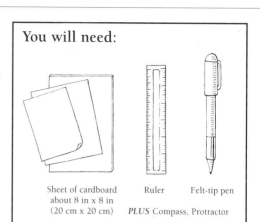

1. Using a compass and a felt-tip pen, draw a circle 6 in (15 cm) in diameter on the cardboard. In its center draw another circle ¾ in (2 cm) in diameter.

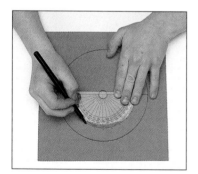

2. Place the center of the protractor on the center of both circles. Mark dots at intervals of 15° all the way around the protractor. Do the same on the other side of the circle. When you are finished, you should have 24 dots altogether.

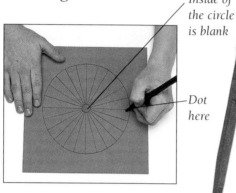

Inside of the circle is blank

Dot here

3. Draw a line connecting each 15° dot to the small circle. Leave the inside of the small circle blank, so you have a pattern like a spoked-wheel. Mark a dot toward the end of the right horizontal spoke, as shown.

Stare straight at the dot with your left eye.

Hold the card at arm's length.

Protractor

Compass

4. Keep your right eye covered and look at the dot with your left eye. Move the card backward and forward until the center circle falls on your blind spot. Instead of vanishing, the center circle is full of spokes. This is because your brain "fills in" the area that the eye does not see with an image that it expects to see. In the case of this experiment, it is a spoked wheel, and not an empty circle.

97 Feel heat

Whenever you sense something, your brain soon adapts to it. Therefore, if you touch something warm, then touch something cool, the cooler object will feel warmer than it really is. Try out this experiment and see if you can fool your temperature receptors.

Adult supervision is advised

You will need:

3 jars

Pitcher of water

1. Fill the jars with cold water, warm water, and hot water (not too hot too touch). Put one finger in the hot water and another finger in the cold water. Hold them there for one minute.

Your brain gradually gets used to the two different temperatures.

2. Now put both fingers in warm water. How does the water feel? Both fingers are in water of the same temperature, but your brain seems to think otherwise. The temperature feels cooler on one finger, and warmer on the other.

98 Test touch

Millions of tiny nerve endings are scattered throughout our skin. With the help of a friend you will discover that different points on your skin are sensitive to different feelings.

You will need:

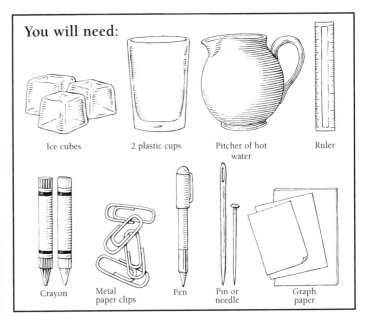

Ice cubes   2 plastic cups   Pitcher of hot water   Ruler

Crayon   Metal paper clips   Pen   Pin or needle   Graph paper

1. Draw a grid of small squares on your hand. Now draw four similar grids on graph paper. Heat one paper clip in hot water; cool another in ice.

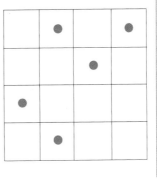

2. Have a friend touch each square of skin with a hot paper clip. Chart on the grid where you can feel the heat of the paper clip.

3. Repeat with the cold paper clip, the crayon, and the pin. On each grid, chart where you feel cold, pressure, and discomfort. Examine the four skin maps. You should find that each square of skin tested felt different sensations.

99 Hidden tastes

Some flavors are so strong that they block out other flavors when present in small amounts. Here is an experiment that you can try on a friend. See how a strong flavor (salt) can mask a weaker flavor (sugar) by testing a friend's sense of taste. Don't tell your friend what is in each glass. See if he or she can guess that there are actually two substances dissolved in the water.

You will need:

4 glasses of water   Teaspoon

Saucer of salt
Saucer of sugar

1. Stir a teaspoon of salt into each glass of water. Now add half a teaspoon of sugar to the first glass, one to the second, one and a half to the third, and two teaspoons to the fourth.

2. Ask your friend to taste the mixture in each glass, starting with the one that has the least sugar. See if they can tell that the water contains something other than salt.

3. Which mixture makes them realize this? Try the experiment on other friends to see if they taste the sugar in different mixtures. Who has the sharpest taste buds?

Salt dissolved in the water

Salt

Sugar

100 Confuse your ears

Having two ears helps you judge where sounds come from. But if the sound is the same distance from both your ears, the sound waves reach them at the same time, and judging is not always easy.

Make sure the blindfold is securely fastened.

1. Put on the blindfold and then sit in a chair. Now ask a friend to snap his or her fingers directly behind, above, or in front of you, but always in line with the center of your body. Can you tell where the sound is coming from every time?

You will need:

Handkerchief   Chair

101 Judge sound direction

Like the experiment on the opposite page, this one shows you how your ears work together. Here, you will find out how good you are at pinpointing sounds that come from many different directions.

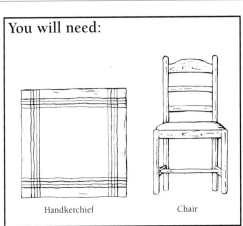
1. Put on a blindfold and then sit on the chair with some of your friends arranged around you in a circle. Ask them to snap their fingers randomly, so you do not know who is going to make the next noise.

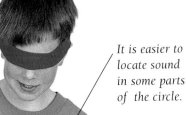

It is easier to locate sound in some parts of the circle.

2. Each time someone snaps, see if you can point to them. Your friends should then tell you if you are right or wrong.

What happens?
Sound reaches one of your ears before the other. Your brain uses this time difference to locate the sound.

95

Index

Acknowledgments

DK would like to thank:
The following children for acting as models: Lia Buddle, Alisdair Cairns, Melissa Chu, Alexandra and Nicholas Denton, Leo Dudley, Ashanti Fearon, William Finnegan, Liam Francis, John Gill, Ben and James Highmore, Patora Ho, Sam Jacobson, Camay Jones, Goran Kanlil, Sharon Lucas, Sophia Nawaz, Lika Razaeince, Alex O'Reilly, Tanisha Russell, Samantha Schneider, Sophie Shannon, Amy and Lucy Smith, and Gemma Taylor. Noltan St. Louis for making the compost box, Martin Smith and Julia Harris for supplying additional props, and Year Four at George Tomlinson School in Leytonstone, London.

Additional special photography: Jane Burton, Peter Chadwick, Andy Crawford, Geoff Dann, Mike Dunning, Steve Gorton, Dave King, Stephen Oliver, Tim Ridley, and Kim Taylor.

Illustrations: Jonathan Wolstenholme
Index: Marion Dent
Picture research: Jo Carlill

With special thanks to David Graham for design assistance

Picture credits
(a = above, b = below, c = center, l = left, r = right, t = top)
Bruce Coleman Limited: 67cra, 70cr
Ron and Christine Foord: 61cr
Frank Lane Picture Agency: 73cl
Harry Smith Collection: 36b

Every effort has been made to trace the copyright holders of photographs, and we apologize for any unavoidable omissions.